GREAT DISCOVERIES IN SCIENCE

Particle Physics

Published in 2019 by Cavendish Square Publishing, LLC
243 5th Avenue, Suite 136, New York, NY 10016

Library of Congress Cataloging-in-Publication Data

Names: Shoup, Kate, 1972- author.
Title: Particle physics / Kate Shoup.
Description: First edition. | New York, NY : Cavendish Square Publishing,
LLC, [2019] | Series: Great discoveries in science | Includes bibliographical references and index. |
Audience: 9 to 12. Identifiers: LCCN 2018013135 (print) | LCCN 2018026077 (ebook) |
ISBN 9781502643711 (ebook) ISBN 9781502643810 (library bound) | ISBN 9781502643933 (pbk.)
Subjects: LCSH: Particles (Nuclear physics)--Juvenile literature. | Particles (Nuclear physics)--Histor--Juvenile literature.
Classification: LCC QC793.27 (ebook) | LCC QC793.27 .S56 2019 (print) | DDC 539.7/2--dc23
LC record available at https://lccn.loc.gov/2018013135

Editorial Director: David McNamara
Editor: Jodyanne Benson
Copy Editor: Michele Suchomel-Casey
Associate Art Director: Alan Sliwinski
Designer: Christina Shults
Production Coordinator: Karol Szymczuk
Photo Research: J8 Media

The photographs in this book are used by permission and through the courtesy of:
Cover, Boscorelli/Shutterstock.com; p. 4 Erik Tham/Corbis/Getty Images; p. 10 De Agostini Picture Library/Getty Images; p. 15 DEA Picture Library/Getty Images; p. 19 1./2. Christie's, LotFinder: entry 5287788 (http://www.christies.com/LotFinder/lot_details.aspx?intObjectID=5287788) (sale 2282, lot 339, New York, 27 January 2010, as Circle of Rembrandt van Rijn) 3. RKD-images, Nr.: 202671 (https://rkd.nl/explore/images/202671)/File: 17th-century Netherlandish artist Democritus with a skull.jpeg/Wikimedia Commons/Public Domain; p. 20 http://wellcomeimages.org/indexplus/obf_images/46/ff/37b5788010996ea730e90a8e50a2.jpg/File: Jabir ibn Hayyan Geber, Arabian alchemist Wellcome L0005558.jpg/Wikimedia Commons/CCA 4.0; p. 22 Frater5 at English Wikipedia/File: Squaredcircle.svg/Wikimedia Commons/Public Domain; p. 27 Science Museum London (https://www.flickr.com/people/98833223@N00)/Science and Society Picture Library (http://www.scienceandsociety.co.uk/)/File: J J Thomsons cathode ray tube with magnet coils, 1897. (9663807404).jpg/Wikimedia Commons/CCA-SA 2.0 Generic; p. 30 Photo Researchers/Science Source/Getty Images; p. 40 Julie Deshaies/Shutterstock.com; p. 43 WIN-Initiative/Getty Images; p. 45 http://wellcomeimages.org/indexplus/obf_images/a2/05/8a3298426a9d4777371c45e4a2da.jpg/File: Portraits of Marie Curie and Pierre Curie Wellcome V0027528.jpg/Wikimedia Commons/CCA 4.0 International; pp. 46, 62, 71 Bettmann/Getty Images; p. 50 Julian Herzog (Website (http://julianherzog.com)/File: CERN LHC Tunnel1.jpg From Wikimedia/Wikimedia Commons/CCA-SA 3.0 Unported; p. 52 Universal History Archive/Getty Images; p. 55 Paul Nadar (1856–1939)/File: Portrait of Antoine-Henri Becquerel.jpg/Wikimedia Commons/Public Domain; p. 65 Elliott & Fry/Hulton Archive/Getty Images; p. 67 Corbis/Getty Images; p. 72 Cush/File: Standard Model of Elementary Particles dark.svg/Wikimedia Commons/CC0 1.0 Universal Public Domain Dedication; p. 85 Peter Macdiarmid/Getty Images; p. 87 SPL/Science Source; p. 89 Jack0m/DigitalVision Vectors/Getty Images; p. 91 Frederic Pitchal/Sygma/Getty Images; p. 94 Alfred Pasieka/Science Photo Library/Getty Images; p. 102 U.S. National Archives and Records Administration/File: Nagasakibomb.jpg/Wikimedia Commons/Public Domain; p. 105 Ragib Hasan (wiki: Ragib Hasan [1] (http://www.ragibhasan.com)/File: Bardeen plaque uiuc.jpg Wikimedia Commons/CCA-SA 2.5 Generic; p. 107ALPA PROD/Shutterstock.com.

Printed in the United States of America

Contents

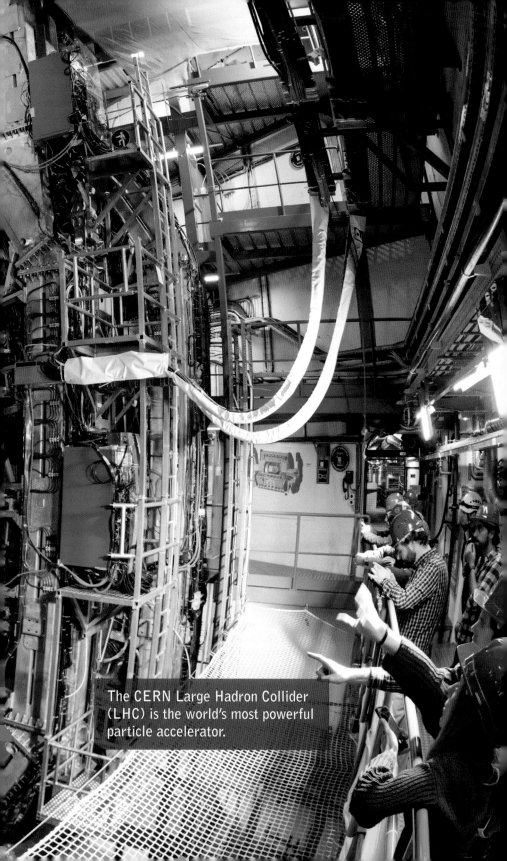

The CERN Large Hadron Collider
(LHC) is the world's most powerful
particle accelerator.

Introduction

I n 1803, a British scientist named John Dalton—building on work by earlier scientists, such as Robert Boyle, Sir Isaac Newton, Gottfried Leibniz, and Ruđer Bošković—put forth a theory on the nature of matter. "Small particles called atoms exist and compose all matter," Dalton wrote. These atoms, he claimed, were "indivisible and indestructible." Finally, Dalton concluded that "Atoms of the same chemical element have the same chemical properties and do not transmute or change into different elements."

For more than ninety years, scientists believed Dalton's model represented the final word on the nature of the atom. Two scientific discoveries during the 1890s, however, proved that aspects of Dalton's model were either wrong or incomplete. The first of these discoveries occurred in 1896, when a French scientist named Henri Becquerel observed a phenomenon we now call radioactive decay. Further study by Becquerel, Marie and Pierre Curie, and Ernest Rutherford would prove that radioactive decay resulted in the transmutation of one element into another. In other words, said Rutherford, "Radioactivity is shown to be accompanied by chemical changes in which new types of matter are being continually produced."

The second discovery to challenge Dalton's atomic model was made by British scientist J. J. Thomson. In 1897, while conducting an experiment involving cathode rays, Thomson determined that atoms contained even smaller parts, meaning they were not in fact indivisible. Indeed, these parts, which Thomson called corpuscles, but scientists later renamed electrons, were *much* smaller than atoms—one hundred million times smaller. Thomson also determined that electrons carried a negative electric charge. This discovery turned the disciplines of chemistry and physics inside out.

Further scientific advancements during the early twentieth century led to a revision of Dalton's atomic model. The most notable of these advancements was the development of an entirely new scientific discipline called quantum physics. This field emerged in 1900 after a German scientist named Max Planck solved a problem, called the blackbody radiation problem, which had bedeviled scientists for decades. Although scientists had hypothesized (and experiments seemed to support) that atoms inside a blackbody should emit energy in a certain way, they had been unable to prove this hypothesis mathematically using the rules of classical physics. Planck discovered that if the equation restricted the amount of energy in these atoms to values of a certain range (rather than all possible values), it could be verified mathematically. From this, Planck and other scientists deduced that rather than being emitted in a gradual manner as had previously been assumed, all energy was emitted in tiny and instantaneous bursts. Moreover, they determined that this energy existed only in unified bundles, which they called quanta (the plural of quantum) and that particles like electrons were types of quanta.

The advent of quantum physics would revolutionize the field of science and lead to many new discoveries. Among these was the discovery of yet more subatomic particles, which would result in a remapping of the atom. For example, in 1911, Rutherford discovered that atoms contained a positively charged mass, which he called the nucleus. In 1921, Rutherford determined that the nucleus contained positively charged particles, which he named protons. In 1932, a British scientist named James Chadwick confirmed the existence of yet another particle, called the neutron. Like the proton, it lived inside the nucleus, but it possessed no electrical charge. Along the way, a Danish scientist named Niels Bohr determined that electrons in atoms circled Rutherford's nucleus in quantized, or fixed, orbits.

Scientists also discovered several elementary particles— that is, particles that truly are the smallest constituent pieces of matter. Collectively, these are called fermions. An electron is a type of fermion. There are also elementary particles associated with certain fundamental forces— collectively called bosons. Scientists have also discovered compound particles, such as baryons and mesons, which are made up of these elementary particles. But that's not all. Scientists have even discovered that most of these subatomic particles have an "evil twin" of sorts in the form of an antiparticle. For example, the antiparticle of an electron is called an antielectron (also known as a positron). When a particle and its antiparticle collide, both are annihilated.

Eventually scientists learned how to manipulate subatomic particles to create new forms of atoms or even force the transmutation of atoms from one chemical element to another. For example, in 1917, Rutherford transmuted nitrogen atoms to oxygen atoms by bombarding them with alpha particles, which consist of two protons and two neutrons. Otto Hahn performed a similar experiment during the 1930s, except he bombarded uranium atoms with neutrons to produce barium and krypton. (This process, called nuclear fission, also freed numerous particles from the uranium atom, including neutrons, and released enormous amounts of energy.)

The study of subatomic particles, their behavior, and the fundamental forces that act on them is called particle physics—sometimes referred to as high-energy physics. Particle physicists keep track of these particles using a framework called the standard model—similar to the periodic table of chemical elements. Particle physicists also use this framework to predict the existence of new particles. The standard model is neither perfect nor complete, however. For example, it does not account for gravity or for mysterious forms of matter and energy called dark matter and dark energy. It also does not explain why the universe has more particles than antiparticles. Scientists hypothesize the existence of several more subatomic particles and antiparticles. For example, they suspect there's such a thing as a graviton, which is a boson associated with the gravitational force, but they have not yet proven its existence.

Interestingly, although the focus in particle physics is on the very small, its implications are universal. In other words, by studying the behavior of these very small particles, particle physicists have been able to understand the nature of our universe and how it was formed. In studying subatomic particles, particle physicists have also learned a great deal about the quantum nature of matter. This includes such odd behaviors as fundamental randomness (which states that there is nothing in nature that dictates whether or how quanta will interact), superposition (which suggests that quanta can exist in more than one location or quantum state at once), quantum entanglement (which occurs when multiple quanta become joined and act as a single quantum), and more. Particle physicists also uncovered the mechanism underpinning radioactivity. (Incidentally, machines that particle physicists have dreamed up to study subatomic particles, such as the particle accelerator, have resulted in the development of revolutionary technologies that touch every aspect of our lives—from medical technologies, to nuclear energy and weaponry, and beyond.)

As far as particle physics has come since J. J. Thomson discovered the electron back in 1897, it still has far to go. Indeed, British physicist Freeman Dyson observes, "we may be as far away from an understanding of elementary particles as Newton's successors were from quantum [physics]." With so much unsettled, particle physics remains a fascinating scientific discipline!

Sir J. J. Thomson (1856–1940) discovered the electron.

CHAPTER 1

Chemistry Through the Ages

P article physics stems from two other scientific disciplines: chemistry and quantum physics. The first of these, chemistry, is the study of the constituent parts of matter and how those parts merge together to form all types of substances and objects. Chemistry has been practiced in one form or another for thousands of years, including metallurgy, alchemy, chemistry, and, eventually, particle physics.

METALLURGY

Members of some of the world's earliest societies grasped that they could manipulate matter—metal in particular— by applying fire (heat). The practice of manipulating metal with heat is called metallurgy. Metallurgy might reasonably be considered the earliest form of chemistry. After all, although early humans may not have realized it, when they applied heat to metal to melt, form, and/or purify it, they were in fact inciting a chemical reaction inside the metal.

(Early humans applied a similar heating technique to ash and crushed quartz to produce glass.)

For millennia humans worked only with "pure" metals. Of these, they knew of only seven, often called the metals of antiquity: gold, silver, copper, lead, tin, iron, and mercury. On their own these metals—generally extracted from ores, which are minerals or rocks that contain metal—were not particularly strong. By 3500 BCE, however, humans had discovered that combining these pure metals could result in the formation of much stronger materials, called alloys.

The first alloy produced by humans was bronze, created by combining copper with tin. Bronze proved so strong it quickly replaced stones as the primary material used to produce tools, weapons, and more. This had a profound effect on early societies. One effect was an increase in trade between regions where tin was scarce and regions where it was abundant. Another effect was a growing power divide between people who could afford bronze implements and those who couldn't. Indeed, the discovery of bronze was so transformative to early human societies that the historical era in which it emerged is now called the Bronze Age.

Around 1200 BCE, societal upheaval in various parts of the world disrupted the tin trade. This left metallurgists with no choice but to devise a replacement for bronze. One candidate was iron. Iron was attractive because it was found in abundance. However, iron had drawbacks, too. Its melting temperature was much higher than that of tin or copper, and it was not particularly strong on its own. Eventually metallurgists discovered that melting iron alongside charcoal produced a crude form of steel.

This crude steel made from iron was not only considerably stronger than bronze, it was also much cheaper to produce. As such, it proved even more transformative to human societies than bronze. Its affordability closed the power divide between the rich and poor, which led to the formation of democratic societies—for example, in ancient Greece. It's no wonder this era was called the Iron Age.

ARISTOTLE'S ELEMENTS

During the Iron Age, philosophers in ancient Greece began pondering the properties and behavior not only of various metals but of other types of matter. Their aim was to explain why different types of matter exhibited different properties (color, density, odor, and so on); why they reacted differently to the application of heat, cold, or liquid; and how they could change from one state to another (solid, liquid, or gas).

Asking questions like these was part of a broader cultural shift to take a more rational approach to understanding the natural world rather than relying on mythology, religion, or the supernatural to explain various natural phenomena. This new approach involved making observations about the natural world and applying those observations to formulate hypotheses and theories about its inner workings.

During the fifth century BCE, a Greek philosopher named Empedocles (490–430 BCE) proposed that all matter was composed of some combination of four simple substances, or elements: earth, water, air, and fire. Empedocles also proposed the existence of two forces, called love and strife, which acted on these elements. Incidentally, the ancient Greeks believed the human body consisted of all four of the earthly elements. They conflated these elements with the four humors: black bile (earth), phlegm (water), blood (air), and yellow bile (fire).

In the fourth century BCE, another Greek philosopher, named Aristotle (384–322 BCE), built on Empedocles's model of matter by proposing that each of the four elements was some combination of hot or cold and dry or wet. The cold elements—earth (cold and dry) and water (cold and wet)—roughly corresponded to our modern conception of solid and liquid, respectively. The warm elements—fire (hot and dry) and air (hot and wet)—matched up with our modern sense of plasma and gas. Aristotle also proposed the existence of a fifth element, called aether (or ether), which he described as the heavenly substance that comprised the stars and planets.

Aristotle also posited that the earth, water, air, and fire elements had a "natural place" toward which they gravitated. These natural places consisted of a series of concentric spheres. The smallest of these was the earth sphere, situated at Earth's center. The water sphere encircled Earth, the air sphere encircled the water sphere, and the fire sphere encircled the air sphere. The placement of these spheres governed the motion of matter. So, matter consisting primarily of earth or water (like rocks or raindrops) would naturally fall downward, toward the two inner spheres, whereas matter made mostly of air or fire (such as air bubbles or fire) would naturally float upward, toward the two outer spheres. Yet another sphere, called the celestial sphere, contained the "heavens."

Greek scholar Aristotle proposed a model of matter that included five elements: earth, water, air, fire, and aether.

Other Early
Interpretations of Matter

The Greeks were not the only ones to posit that earth, water, air, fire, and aether (the material that fills the region of the universe above the earthly sphere) comprised the basic elements of matter. Philosophers in Egypt, Babylonia, the Mayan civilization, Japan, India, and Tibet put forth similar hypotheses. However, these philosophers sometimes used slightly different nomenclature. For example, they would refer to air as wind and to aether as space or a void.

They also held somewhat different views on how these elements behaved. Ancient Egyptians, for instance, believed living things were either "friends" or "enemies" of certain elements. One ancient text explains: "The locust and all flies flee fire; the eagle and the hawk and all high-flying birds flee water; fish, air and earth; the snake avoids the open air. Whereas snakes and all creeping things love earth; all swimming things love water; winged things, air, of which they are the citizens; while those that fly still higher love the fire and have the habitat near it."

Chinese philosophers, on the other hand, put forth a slightly different model. This model maintained that earth, water, and fire were fundamental elements, but air and aether were replaced by wood and metal. The model put forth by Chinese philosophers also presented these elements not so much as different types of materials but rather as different types of energy that acted on each other in a rock-paper-scissor fashion.

For example, in a cycle called the generating cycle, wood fed fire, fire created earth (ash), earth bore metal, metal collected water, and water nourished wood. In another cycle called the overcoming cycle, wood parted earth, earth absorbed water, water quenched fire, fire melted metal, and metal chopped wood.

ATOMISM

Aristotle's model of matter differed sharply from another model put forth around the same time by a Greek philosopher named Leucippus (fifth century BCE) and his student Democritus (460–370 BCE). According to this theory, called atomism, all matter consisted of tiny particles called *a-tomos* (meaning "not able to be cut" or "without parts"). An a-tomo, which represented the smallest possible particle of a given piece of matter, was both indivisible and indestructible. The contents of all a-tomos were identical, but their size, shape, mass, position, and arrangement could vary. These variations dictated what type of matter a given a-tomo was.

According to Leucippus and Democritus, a-tomos flew in straight lines in all directions through empty space, which they called the void. The resulting collisions, caroms, and entanglements were the basis of all that occurred in the material world. Democritus went one step further by suggesting that not only were a-tomos the basis of all that occurred in the material world, they (along with the void) were all that existed in the material world. "By convention sweet is sweet, by convention bitter is bitter, by convention hot is hot, by convention cold is cold, by convention color is color," Democritus wrote. "But in reality, there are a-tomos and the void. That is, the objects of sense are supposed to be real and it is customary to regard them as such, but in truth they are not. Only the a-tomos and the void are real."

Aristotle vehemently rejected atomism. He did not deny the possibility that a substance could be subdivided into its smallest possible parts. These smallest parts were called the

Democritus with a Skull (c. 1600s) was painted by the school of Jan Cossiers.

minimum naturalia. But he argued against the notion that these tiny parts were indivisible. He also contended that the existence of a void was impossible.

ALCHEMY

In 146 BCE, the Roman Empire absorbed the Greek Empire. More than six hundred years later, in 476 CE, the Roman Empire collapsed. Chaos engulfed western Europe, ultimately cutting off nearly all communication between its inhabitants and their neighbors to the east.

Muslim scholar Abu Mūsā Jābir ibn Hayyān (721–815 CE) was a Muslim scholar who studied chemistry, alchemy, astronomy, and philosophy.

During this period, much of the scientific knowledge gleaned by the ancient Greeks was lost—at least to western Europeans. It was not lost everywhere, however. Volumes of scientific texts written by the ancient Greeks fell under the care of citizens of the Byzantine Empire. Later, Muslim scholars throughout Byzantium—which at that time covered the Balkan Peninsula in eastern Europe, modern-day Turkey, parts of central Asia and the Middle East, and northern Africa—translated these texts into Arabic and built on the knowledge they imparted.

One such Muslim scholar was Abu Mūsā Jābir ibn Hayyān (721–815 CE). Jabir built on Aristotle's model of matter to include two additional "philosophical" elements, sulfur and mercury, which he believed worked together to produce all metals. Jābir also organized matter into three categories: metals; spirits, which vaporized when heated; and substances such as stones that could be ground into powders. Finally, Jābir applied to this model the principles of numerology, which ascribe divine or mystical qualities to numbers, to define the nature and properties of each element. Jābir believed that within this framework it was possible to transform one metal into another and perhaps even create life.

Starting in the eleventh century, communication between western Europeans and their Byzantine neighbors increased. This was due primarily to a series of battles called the Crusades between Christian soldiers in Europe and their Muslim counterparts in Byzantium. The Crusades exposed European soldiers to a wealth of goods from the East they had never dreamed existed, which in turn resulted in the development of trade relations between the two regions.

Europeans and the Byzantines didn't just trade goods, however. They also traded knowledge and ideas, including knowledge and ideas gleaned by ancient Greek scholars and their Byzantine successors.

Among the ideas that drifted back to western Europe in the aftermath of the Crusades was Jābir's model of matter. Medieval philosophers in western Europe (as well as in

The philosopher's stone is represented by this alchemical symbol.

India and the Middle East) quickly adopted this model and incorporated it into a new field of study they called alchemy.

Most alchemists in western Europe shared a single goal: to produce a philosopher's stone, which they believed could be used to transform so-called "base metals," such as lead or mercury, into "noble metals," like gold. Alchemists referred to the process of this transformation as *chrysopoeia*, from the Greek *khrusos*, meaning "gold," and *poiēin*, meaning "to make." It was said that a philosopher's stone could also serve as an elixir of life that both cured disease and bestowed immortality. It could also serve as a universal solvent.

Over time alchemy took on a mystical quality, guided more by magic and mythology than by science. Eventually alchemy's mysticism shifted to something darker: fraudulence. This explains why in his famous *Inferno*, Italian poet Dante Alighieri (1265–1321) consigned alchemists to the tenth circle of hell along with other so-called "falsifiers," including counterfeiters and bearers of false witness. Their punishment was to live for eternity covered in scabs, their bodies corrupted by disease in the same way they corrupted society.

The SCIENTIFIC REVOLUTION

In 1453, the Ottoman Empire conquered Byzantium, prompting many Byzantine scholars to flee westward. Suddenly the gentle stream of knowledge from Byzantium to Europe that had begun in the aftermath of the Crusades became a flood.

The effect of this flood was two-fold. First, it ushered in an era of incredible scientific discovery by

European scholars, called the Scientific Revolution. Second, and perhaps more important, it introduced European scholars to the Greek method of scientific inquiry. Suddenly, European scholars, like their Greek predecessors, began relying more on formulating hypotheses and theories based on careful observation and less on mythology, religion, and the supernatural to improve their understanding of the natural world.

During this period, alchemy eventually gave way to another discipline called chemistry. Chemistry is the study of the composition, structure, and properties of substances. It also examines the transformations these substances undergo.

The REDISCOVERY of the ATOM

Alchemists adopted the Aristotelian model of matter (as interpreted by Jābir) rather than the atomic model proposed by Leucippus and Democritus. During the Scientific Revolution, however, scientists did the opposite, abandoning the Aristotelian model for one more like atomism.

One of these scientists was Robert Boyle (1627–1691). In his book *The Sceptical Chymist,* published in 1661, Boyle posited that bodies consisted of "parts very minute and of differing figures," that "there does also intervene a various local motion of such small bodies," that the "smallest and neighbouring" particles "were here and there associated into minute masses or clusters," and that these masses and clusters "were not easily dissipable into such particles as composed them." In other words, matter was made of tiny particles that were subject to motion. These particles clumped together to form masses, and these masses were difficult to divide.

Boyle also described what he called "elements" as "certain primitive and simple, or perfectly unmingled bodies; which not being made of any other bodies, or of one another, are the ingredients of all those called perfectly mixed bodies are immediately compounded, and into which they are ultimately resolved." Put another way, he saw elements as primitive, simple, and pure; as the ingredients that, when compounded, constituted matter; and as the ingredients into which matter ultimately broke down. (Boyle is also famous for his articulation of Boyle's law, which defines the relationship between pressure and gas.)

Sir Isaac Newton (1643–1727) was another scientist who took an interest in the fundamental composition of matter. In a book called *Opticks*, published in 1704, Newton proposed that matter was made of "solid, massy, hard, impenetrable, moveable particles" formed by God. "These primitive particles being solids," he explained, "are incomparably harder than any porous bodies compounded of them; even so very hard as never to wear or break in pieces: no ordinary power being able to divide what God himself made one in the first Creation."

Ultimately, these particles, which Newton called corpuscles, were not unlike the a-tomos envisioned by the early Greeks. Unlike a-tomos, however, corpuscles could conceivably be divided into even smaller particles but still retain all their characteristics and could attract other similar particles at close range. Newton's corpuscle model is widely viewed as the predecessor of our modern model of the atom.

In 1714, a German scientist named Gottfried Leibniz (1646–1716) developed an alternative model for the atom, which he called a monad. Leibniz described monads as "the elements out of which everything is made" and believed "every monad is a mirror of the universe in its own way." Apart from asserting that each monad was a tiny point of energy and contained no smaller parts, Leibniz declined to describe the physical structure of the nomad in detail.

He did describe its three key qualities, however. First, monads were unified. They could not be divided. This meant that the only way monads came into or went out of existence was instantaneously: "being created or annihilated all at once." Second, each monad was "qualitatively unlike every other." Third, monads underwent constant change (both structural and behavioral), and this change could result only from the application of internal (rather than external) forces.

During the mid-1700s, Croatian mathematician Ruđer Bošković (1711–1787) combined Newton's sense of corpuscles as elementary particles that could attract at close distances with Leibniz's view of monads as points of energy to create a new atomic theory. Bošković's theory suggested that matter was made of points, called atom points, surrounded by fields with positive and negative charges. These atom points could both attract (at short distances) and repel (from farther away) other atom points. Atom points could also combine to form both chemical elements and compounds made of these elements. The chemical composition of these elements and compounds was the result of the pattern of the fields surrounding the atom points.

While these and other scientists contributed to our modern understanding of the atom, history credits a British scientist named John Dalton (1766–1844) with its actual identification. Dalton concluded in 1803 that all matter was made of microscopic particles called atoms and that atoms were both indivisible and indestructible. In other words, they were the smallest possible piece of matter.

Dalton also determined that all atoms of a given chemical element—such as hydrogen, oxygen, nitrogen, etc.—were identical in mass and properties. In other words, each chemical element had its own unique type of atom. Dalton then deduced that compounds were formed by a combination of two or more different kinds of atoms. (We call these molecules.) Finally, Dalton ascertained that a chemical reaction is in fact a rearrangement of atoms.

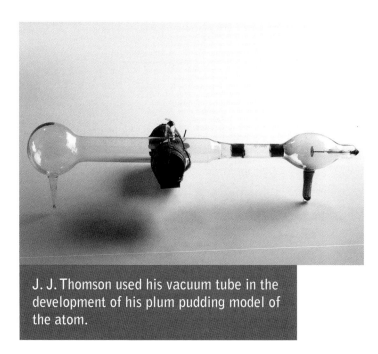

J. J. Thomson used his vacuum tube in the development of his plum pudding model of the atom.

The DISCOVERY of the ELECTRON

Dalton's atomic model, which endured for nearly a century, posited that atoms were the smallest possible pieces of matter. His model was not completely new in the sense that the ancient Greeks had also posited that all matter is composed of small, indivisible (cannot be divided) objects. However, in 1897, a scientist named Sir J. J. Thomson (1856–1940) proved Dalton wrong.

Thomson hadn't set out to challenge Dalton's model of the atom. He was simply trying to explain something that occurred when scientists applied voltage to two electrodes on either end of a vacuum tube—one connected to the positive terminal of the voltage supply (called an anode) and the other to the negative terminal (called a cathode). Specifically, applying voltage caused a visible ray of energy, called a cathode ray, to stream from the cathode end of the tube to the anode end.

Scientists had no idea what this ray was made of. Some held that they were, in Thomson's words, "due to some process in the aether to which … no phenomenon hitherto observed is analogous. Others, he said, believed "that, so far from being wholly aetherial, they are in fact wholly material, and that they mark the paths of particles of matter charged with negative electricity."

Through experimentation Thomson concluded that this latter view was correct. But he took it a step further, positing that these particles, which he called primordial atoms (later renamed electrons), represented "matter in a new state … in which the subdivision of matter is carried very much further than [before]" and that they were "the substance from which all the chemical elements are built up." In other words, electrons were subatomic particles. They existed inside atoms.

Thomson also found electrons to be identical to each other and infinitesimal in size. He ultimately concluded that atoms consisted of negatively charged electrons embedded inside a substance that was positively charged (to balance out the negatively charged electrons). This model came to be pictured like a plum pudding: the negatively charged "plums" are surrounded by positively charged "pudding." Hence, Thomson's model became known as the plum pudding model.

The electron would prove to be just one of several subatomic particles discovered by scientists. These particles are the focus of the scientific discipline of particle physics. In the next chapter, we will explore the foundation of particle physics. We will take a closer look at the discovery of subatomic particles as well as the development of the standard model.

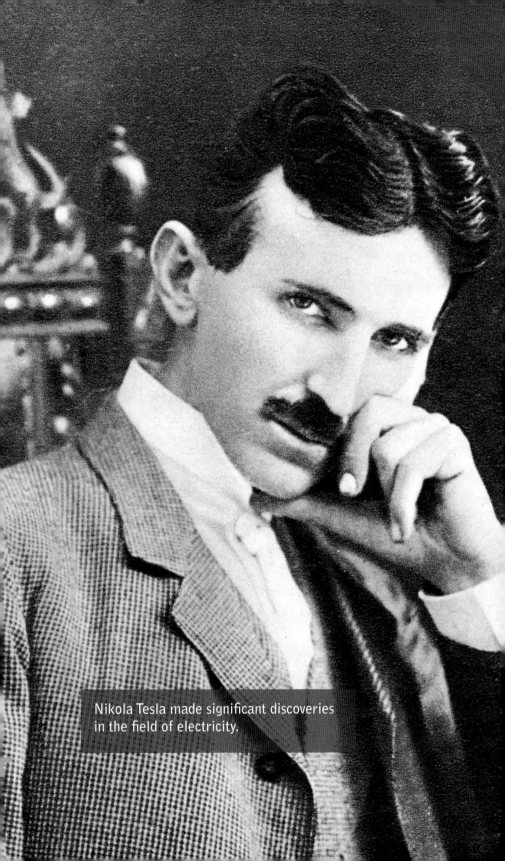

Nikola Tesla made significant discoveries in the field of electricity.

CHAPTER 2

The Foundation of Particle Physics

The seminal discovery of particle physics, Sir J. J. Thomson's discovery of the electron in 1897, was predicated on several earlier scientific developments. For example, to conduct the experiment that revealed the existence of the electron, Thomson needed an understanding of Dalton's atomic model (discussed in chapter 1), vacuum, electricity (including positive and negative charges), and fields.

The subsequent discovery of additional subatomic particles and their assembly into a framework called the standard model, which serves as the foundation of particle physics, would require still more advancements in science. These included the identification and classification of various chemical elements (including radioactive elements) and the development of an entirely new scientific discipline called quantum physics.

The SCIENTIFIC METHOD

Scientists investigate the world, make discoveries, and draw conclusions by using a specific methodology. This method, first developed by Sir Francis Bacon (1561–1626) during the early 1600s, is called the scientific method, and it remains in use today.

Bacon's scientific method placed special importance on experimentation. As he wrote in his *Novum Organum* (1620), "There remains simple experience; which, if taken as it comes, is called accident, if sought for, experiment." Bacon continued, "The true method of experience first lights the candle [hypothesis], and then by means of the candle shows the way [arranges and delimits the experiment]; commencing as it does with experience duly ordered and digested, not bungling or erratic, and from it deducing axioms [theories], and from established axioms again new experiments."

The modern scientific method includes many of these same steps: making observations; developing questions about the observations; formulating a hypothesis about the observations; developing predictions; gathering data (through experimentation and/or the application of mathematics) to test the predictions; refining, altering, expanding, or rejecting the hypothesis; developing a general theory; and beginning the cycle anew. By using the scientific method, scientists ensure their approach to scientific inquiry is rigorous. They also increase the likelihood that the general theories they develop are correct.

The scientific method reflects a key tenet of scientific study: scientific ideas evolve as the result of new observations and discoveries. This method also appeals to rational thought, experimentation, and mathematics to verify whether the conclusion is true. The possibility always remains that a new theory, experiment, or discovery could emerge.

SETTLING the VACUUM DISPUTE

Philosophers and scientists have debated the existence of vacuum for thousands of years. Greek philosophers like Leucippus and Democritus believed vacuum, which they called void, did exist. Aristotle disagreed, famously declaring that "nature abhors a vacuum." In 1643, an Italian scientist named Evangelista Torricelli (1608–1647) settled the matter once and for all by producing a vacuum in his laboratory, albeit a partial one.

A vacuum (from the Latin *vacuus*, meaning "vacant" or "void")—or, more precisely, a perfect vacuum—is a region of space completely devoid of air or other gas and therefore of pressure. A partial vacuum, like the one Torricelli produced, is a region of space whose pressure is lower than the atmospheric pressure.

Objects in a vacuum, whether that vacuum is perfect or partial, behave differently from objects outside a vacuum. For example, if one were to create a vacuum in a tube, stand the tube on its end, and insert a feather into the top of the tube, the feather would not float downward. Rather, it would plummet, the same way a rock does.

Scientists perform many types of experiments using vacuum, including experiments meant to simulate conditions in outer space.

UNDERSTANDING ELECTRICITY

Even in ancient times, people had some awareness of the existence of electricity—primarily through contact with fish such as the electric eel. They also had some experience with static electricity, having noticed that rubbing amber on fur could attract certain lightweight objects such as feathers. But it wasn't until the late 1500s that electricity became a serious subject of scientific inquiry in the Western world.

A British scientist named William Gilbert (1544–1603) was among the first to differentiate electricity (which produced the interaction between amber and fur) from magnetism (evident when one object was naturally drawn to another due to inherent properties in each). Gilbert also coined a new Latin term *electricus* (from *elektron*, the Greek word for "amber") to describe this phenomenon.

During the 1700s, American scholar and statesman Benjamin Franklin (1706–1790) observed that electricity involved two types of charges: positive and negative. Objects with a positive charge attracted objects with a negative charge (and vice versa). However, two objects with the same charge—positive or negative—repelled each other.

During the 1800s, scientists developed an excellent understanding of how electricity worked. For example, they discovered that electrical charges could move, and when they did, they were said to create a current. The lightbulb invented by Thomas Edison (1847–1941) in 1879 worked using one type of current, called direct current, identified by Italian physicist Alessandro Volta (1745–1827) in 1800. Another type of current, called alternating current, was identified by Serbian physicist Nikola Tesla (1856–1943) during the 1880s. Finally, they determined that current could follow a particular path, which they called a circuit. Scientists also identified substances through which current could flow more easily, which they called conductors, as well as substances that blocked the flow of current, called insulators. When insulators blocked current, they were said to produce resistance—the electrical equivalent to friction. These discoveries ushered in an era of tremendous innovation and invention, including the electric battery, telegraph, telephone, lightbulb, and other important technologies.

IDENTIFYING FIELDS

Prior to the mid-1800s scientists believed the universe consisted of atoms moving through empty space and interacting only through direct contact or direct action. However, a self-taught scientist named Michael Faraday (1791–1867) perceived one key weakness in this model: it failed to account for the behavior of magnets, which could pull iron—and could push or pull other magnets— without direct contact or action. Faraday determined that the presence of a magnet altered the space around it, and this alteration, which Faraday called a magnetic field, was a characteristic, or property, of space itself. (Later scientists realized the magnetic field was in fact the same phenomenon as another field, called the electrical field. They now describe both fields together as the electromagnetic field.) In other words, Faraday proved that space was not empty. Faraday also concluded that forces like magnetism and electricity existed not in objects but in space itself.

Faraday was very intelligent, but his mathematical skills were limited. In 1865, a physicist named

James Clerk Maxwell (1831–1879) published a treatise
called *A Dynamical Theory of the Electromagnetic Field.*
This summarized Faraday's work into a comprehensive
set of differential equations that described the behavior
of electromagnetic fields and served as the foundation for
all modern theories pertaining to electromagnetism. It
also predicted the existence of electromagnetic waves that
moved at or near the speed of light. According to Maxwell,
visible light rays as well as invisible rays such as infrared
(discovered in 1800) and ultraviolet (identified in 1801) were
all examples of electromagnetic waves.

The IDENTIFICATION and CLASSIFICATION of CHEMICAL ELEMENTS

As noted in chapter 1, Aristotle believed that all of matter was
made of some combination of earth, water, air, fire, and aether.
During the 1600s, a scientist named Robert Boyle challenged
this view. Boyle believed the real elements were those elements
that could not be decomposed into a simpler substance. Boyle's
view has prevailed. Today we know that a chemical element is
a substance that contains only one kind of atom.

During Boyle's time, relatively few elements had been
discovered—and none through scientific means. These
included the seven metals of antiquity (gold, silver, copper,
lead, tin, iron, and mercury); carbon (discovered circa 3750
BCE); sulfur (2000 BCE); zinc (1000 BCE); arsenic (300 CE);
and antimony (800 CE).

The first element discovered in a laboratory was
phosphorus, by German alchemist Hennig Brand

(1630–1692 or 1710) in 1669. Brand made this discovery
by conducting an experiment that involved boiling urine.
Next came cobalt (1735), platinum (1748), nickel (1751),
bismuth (1753), and magnesium (1755). By 1789, scientists
had identified thirty-three chemical elements, including
hydrogen (1766), oxygen (1771), and nitrogen (1772).
As of today, scientists have observed 118 elements. Of
these, ninety-eight can be found in nature; the rest were
synthesized in a lab.

In 1811, Italian chemist Amedeo Avogadro
(1776–1856) correctly observed that the atoms of one
chemical element could bond with the atoms of another
chemical element to form what he called a molecule. These
molecules combined to form a wholly new substance called
a chemical compound.

In 1830, Michael Faraday theorized that some atoms
and molecules could possess a positive or negative electrical
charge. He called these charged atoms and molecules ions.
Ions with a positive charge were called cations, and ions
with a negative charge were called anions. Ionized atoms
or molecules would behave quite differently than their
standard counterparts—becoming attracted to matter
with the opposite charge; repelled by matter with the same
charge; and subject to forces in magnetic fields. Today we
know that ions do indeed exist and that they are formed
when an atom or molecule gains or loses an electron
through some type of chemical process.

Around this same time scientists discovered that atoms
and molecules could exist as other forms. For example,
in 1827, a German chemist named Friedrich Woehler
(1800–1882) discovered that two molecules containing

Dmitry Mendeleyev

The youngest of seventeen children, Dmitry Mendeleyev was born on February 8, 1834, near Tobolsk, in Siberia. He is a well-known chemist and inventor. Specifically, he is known for creating the periodic table.

When Mendeleyev was very young, his father, a schoolteacher, went blind and lost his job. He died in 1847. Mendeleyev's mother, Maria, who hailed from a prominent merchant family, opened a glass factory to support the family. Sadly, the factory burned down in 1848.

In 1848, Mendeleyev moved to St. Petersburg, Russia, to study science at St. Petersburg University. Afterward, he accepted a research post in Heidelberg, Germany, and published an award-winning textbook on organic chemistry. In 1865, Mendeleyev returned to St. Petersburg University, where he earned his doctorate the same year. He remained there in a professorial capacity until 1890.

In 1862, Mendeleyev married Feozva Nikitichna Leshcheva, but he abandoned her for another woman, Anna Ivanova Popova, in 1882. Russian society was scandalized, which explains why despite his accomplishments, he was never admitted to the Russian Academy of Sciences.

Developing the periodic table was not Mendeleyev's only scientific contribution. Russian chemist Lev Chugaev (1873–1922) described Mendeleyev as "a chemist of genius, first-class physicist, a fruitful researcher in the fields of hydrodynamics, meteorology, geology, certain branches of chemical technology (explosives, petroleum, and fuels, for example) and other disciplines adjacent to chemistry and physics, a thorough expert of chemical industry and industry in general, and an original thinker in the field of economy."

Mendeleyev died of influenza in St. Petersburg, on February 2, 1907. He was seventy-two years old. In 1955, scientists named a newly discovered element, mendelevium, in his honor.

PERIODIC TABLE OF THE ELEMENTS

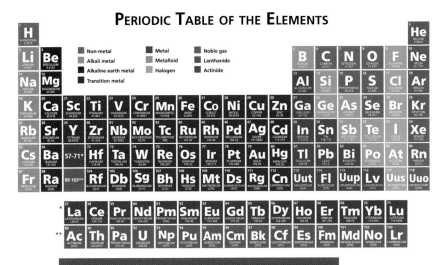

The modern periodic table of the elements orders the chemical elements by their atomic number.

the exact same atoms could possess different properties depending on how the atoms were arranged. Such a molecule was called an isomer. In 1841, a Swedish scientist named Baron Jöns Jacob Berzelius (1779–1848) proposed the concept of the allotrope, which is a variant form of a chemical element or molecular substance. By 1860, this concept was widely accepted. Scientists concluded that some molecular allotropes were simply molecules composed of two or more atoms of a particular element, such as dioxygen (which constitutes more than 20 percent of Earth's atmosphere). Other allotropes are the result of differences in an element's physical structure—for example, in the case of a diamond, which is an allotrope of carbon.

Of course, scientists had long observed that matter— in other words, chemical elements and chemical compounds—existed in three forms: solid, gas, and liquid. Matter in solid form maintained a fixed volume and shape. Matter in liquid form maintained a fixed volume but was variable in shape depending on its container. Finally, matter in gas form was variable in both volume and shape—again, depending on its container. During the 1800s, scientists determined that these states reflected how tightly the atoms in a substance were packed together. A substance whose atoms were packed together very tightly would present as a solid; one whose atoms were very loosely packed would present as a gas; and one whose atoms were packed somewhere in between would present as a liquid. Scientists also determined that matter switched from one of these states to another through the application (or removal) of energy—usually in thermal form.

During the 1860s, a Russian scientist named Dmitry Mendeleyev (1834–1907) noticed that certain chemical elements seemed to share similar properties. In 1869, using these shared properties as his guide, Mendeleyev organized the chemical elements known at that time into a chart called the periodic table. This table listed all elements from smallest to largest (based on their mass) and grouped all elements with similar properties into columns. Building on a notation system developed by Berzelius in 1808, Mendeleyev represented each element using a one- or two-letter abbreviation of its Latin name—for example, "Fe" for ferrum, the Latin name for iron. Identifying gaps in the periodic table enabled Mendeleyev to correctly predict the existence of several more elements. By the mid-1880s, Mendeleyev's table had won wide acceptance among scientists. Today, Mendeleyev's table has expanded to include 118 chemical elements, organized into eighteen groups.

The OBSERVATION of RADIOACTIVITY

In 1896, a French physicist named Henri Becquerel (1852–1908), whose research centered on a phenomenon called phosphorescence (the glow that some chemical elements emit long after they have absorbed energy from an outside energy source, such as sunlight) sought to determine whether X-rays were the source of that glow. To find out, he developed an experiment that involved wrapping a photographic plate with opaque paper, placing a chunk of uranium salt (which phosphoresces when exposed to light) on the plate, and placing the plate outside in the sun for several hours. As he expected, the uranium salts absorbed the light and emitted sufficient radiation to expose the photographic plate. The following week, however, he discovered that the uranium salts emitted sufficient radiation to expose the photographic plate even if they hadn't been exposed to sunlight. In other words, it seemed that the uranium cast off energy all by itself—and lots of it.

In 1897, a Polish scientist working in France named Marie Skłodowska Curie (1867–1934) began studying this phenomenon. Assisted by her husband, Pierre, Marie discovered that the energy emitted by uranium remained consistent regardless of the element's condition or form.

Henri Becquerel (1852–1908) focused his research on a phenomenon called phosphorescence, which is the glow that some chemical elements emit long after they have absorbed energy from an outside energy source.

From this, Marie concluded "that the emission of [energy] by the compounds of uranium is a property of the metal itself—that it is an atomic property of the element uranium independent of its chemical or physical state." In other words, the atom emitted energy all by itself—not in response to some outside stimulus, such as the application of heat. To describe this phenomenon, Marie coined the term "radioactivity."

During the early 1900s, two British scientists, Ernest Rutherford (1871–1937) and Frederick Soddy (1877–1956), concluded that radioactivity occurred when an atom broke down—a process they called radioactive decay. The result of radioactive decay was the formation of an atom of a different element. Rutherford also determined that this decay occurred over a predictable period to a point of stability, called a half-life. Depending on the element, this period could span from fractions of a second to trillions of years. The energy emitted from radioactive atoms was first described as rays but later as particles. There were three types of these particles: alpha particles, beta particles, and gamma particles. Each of these particles was the result of a different type of radioactive decay, called alpha decay, beta decay, and gamma decay.

What Becquerel, the Curies, Rutherford, and Soddy didn't understand, at least right away, was the driving mechanism behind radioactive decay. That would come later, after the discovery of quantum physics.

Marie Curie

Pierre Curie

Marie Curie, and her husband, Pierre, made important discoveries in the field of radioactivity.

Max Planck is widely viewed as the father of quantum physics.

The QUANTUM UNIVERSE

During the closing years of the nineteenth century, scientists believed they completely understood the inner workings of the universe. They saw it as rather like a mechanical clock: entirely predictable. All that was left, they supposed, was to improve methodologies and seek more accurate methods of measurement.

At the turn of the twentieth century, however, they discovered something new. This occurred after scientists noticed certain natural phenomena they could not explain. One such phenomenon was called the blackbody radiation problem. A blackbody is a theoretical "perfect" surface.

Scientists hypothesized (and experiments seemed to support) that while in a state of equilibrium, a blackbody would both absorb and emit all frequencies, or wavelengths, of the electromagnetic spectrum—from gamma rays to visible light to microwaves to ultra-low frequency waves and everything in between. But they were unable to explain this phenomenon or prove it mathematically.

In December 1900, a German mathematician named Max Planck (1858–1947) posited that the radiation emitted by a blackbody was the result of energy released by atoms vibrating inside it. As Planck attempted to compose an equation to prove this hypothesis, he grew increasingly frustrated. Finally, he concluded that the math would be simpler if he assumed that the amount of energy released by these atoms was restricted to values of a certain range rather than allowed any arbitrary value. Planck, in what he called "an act of desperation," decided to first solve the equation using these ranges, or increments, and figure out how to adjust the equation to accommodate all values later. The problem was, Planck's equation couldn't accommodate all values. It could only accommodate the incremental ones.

At first, Planck had no idea why his equation worked the way it did. Eventually, he grasped that the fact that his equation could accommodate incremental values but not all values indicated that the energy emitted by the vibrating atoms in blackbody radiation was quantized rather than continuous. That is, rather than being emitted in a gradual manner, this energy—indeed, all energy—was emitted in tiny and instantaneous bursts.

From this, scientists concluded that energy existed only in unified bundles, called quanta (the singular form of quantum, from the Latin *quantus*, meaning "how many"). This discovery formed the foundation of a new and important field of scientific study called quantum physics. Physicists believe quanta comprise everything in the universe, including subatomic particles.

Quanta exhibit some interesting characteristics. One is that they either exist in their entirety, or they don't exist at all. They are created or destroyed all at once, and they cannot be divided. Another is that although they sometimes act like particles, they are in fact waves. Given the nature of waves, the precise position and velocity of a quantum cannot be precisely measured. This means that quantum physics in not a deterministic framework in which the universe is wholly predictable. Rather, it is a probabilistic framework. This is significant because it suggests the universe is fundamentally random: there is absolutely nothing in nature that dictates whether one quantum will interact with another, and if two (or more) quanta do interact, there is absolutely nothing in nature that dictates what the outcome of that interaction will be.

A third characteristic of quanta is that they can exist in various quantum states. They can be infinitesimal or enormous; they can shrink or expand; they contain lots of energy or not so much; they can exist at any location; and they can move in any direction. They can also, and this is strange, exist in two or more of these opposing states at the same time. This phenomenon is called superposition, and although it sounds a little odd, scientists have observed this phenomenon at the subatomic level.

Superposition is not the only odd behavior observed in quantum physics. Another is quantum entanglement. This occurs when two (or more) quanta become joined together and behave much like a single unified quantum. In other words, when two quanta are entangled, the state of one quantum will exactly match the state of the other. Moreover, if the state of one of these quanta changes, the state of the other will, too—instantaneously.

Odd behaviors like superposition and quantum entanglement can be observed only in very small matter, like atoms and electrons. This fact—along with advances in our understanding of the atom (themselves gleaned through quantum physics)—revealed the need for a new field of study: particle physics.

QUANTUM CONUNDRUMS

Quantum physics describes behavior that seems contrary to that observed in the "real" world. Consider superposition. You've probably never seen an object assume multiple

The Large Hadron Collider (LHC) allows scientists to confirm the existence of theoretical subatomic particles.

states—for example, moving along multiple paths—at once. So, you'd reasonably assume it would be impossible for a quantum to do so. Yet, a quantum can assume multiple states—including moving along multiple paths—simultaneously. Indeed, scientists have shown that it does.

Some ideas that scientists come up with seem unbelievable, at least initially. The scientific method prevents scientists from calling these ideas "fact" without proof, which comes through rigorous experimentation and testing. Scientists are also guided by a principle called Occam's razor. This principle states that when faced with a scientific problem, such as the behavior of a quantum, one should accept the simplest explanation. If through observation and experimentation one concludes that the simplest explanation is not correct, one should pursue the next-simplest answer, and so on. So, for a scientific conundrum such as the behavior of a quantum, scientists argue that a quantum can move along multiple paths simultaneously. They arrived at this conclusion because the simpler explanations could not be verified.

This photograph shows the Cavendish Laboratory researchers in 1928.

CHAPTER 3

Key Contributors to the Field of Particle Physics

M any scientists contributed to the early development of particle physics. This chapter introduces several of these scientists: Henri Becquerel, J. J. Thomson, Marie Skłodowska Curie, Ernest Rutherford, Niels Bohr, James Chadwick, Otto Hahn, and Richard Feynman.

These physicists had much in common. Many of them studied or taught at the same institutions—for example, Thomson, Rutherford, and Chadwick all studied at Cambridge University, in England. Some taught each other: Thomson taught Rutherford, and Rutherford taught Hahn and Chadwick. Many of them collaborated in their work, such as Henri Becquerel and Marie Curie, and Ernest Rutherford and Niels Bohr (who also became great friends). All of them won a Nobel Prize—some in physics, some in chemistry, and some, like Marie Curie, in both. The achievements of these scientists, and their contributions to particle physics, cannot be overstated.

HENRI BECQUEREL (1852–1908)

Henri Becquerel was the first person to observe radioactive behavior. The becquerel (Bq), a unit of radioactivity, is named for him, as is a uranium-based mineral called becquerelite.

Becquerel was born on December 15, 1852, in Paris, France. He was the only child of Aurélie and Alexandre-Edmond Becquerel. The Becquerels were a well-to-do and well-respected family. Becquerel's father was a distinguished scholar who conducted research on solar radiation and phosphorescence. His grandfather, Antoine Cesar Becquerel, was also a scientist. He invented a method to extract metals from ore.

Becquerel received his early schooling at the prestigious Lycée Louis-le-Grand, in Paris. Starting in 1872, Becquerel pursued a two-year course of scientific study at the École Polytechnique. Following that he studied engineering at the École des Ponts et Chaussées, finishing his degree in 1877.

Starting in 1876, Becquerel began working at the École Polytechnique—first as an assistant and finally as the chair of the Physics Department. He also worked at the Muséum National d'Histoire Naturelle starting in 1878, at the Paris Museum starting in 1892, and for the French Department of Bridges and Highways. In 1889, he was elected a member of the Académie des Sciences de France, an organization committed to the advancement of science in France.

In 1874, Becquerel married Lucie Jamin, whose father was an engineer. Sadly, Lucie died shortly after giving birth to a son, Jean, in 1878. Jean would grow up to be a scientist just like his father, grandfather, and great-grandfather before

Henri Becquerel was the first scientist to observe a phenomenon Marie Curie would later call radiation.

him. Twelve years later Becquerel married again—this time to Louise Lorieux.

Becquerel discovered radioactivity quite by accident while conducting an experiment to determine whether phosphorescence might be related to X-rays. This discovery would alter his career path and even earn him a Nobel Prize for Physics in 1903—an honor he shared with Marie and Pierre Curie.

Henri Becquerel died in Le Croisic, France, on August 25, 1908. He was fifty-five years old. His cause of death is unknown. However, based on the presence of serious burns and scars on his skin, historians speculate it may have been related to his unsafe handling of radioactive materials.

MARIE SKŁODOWSKA CURIE (1867–1934)

Marie Skłodowska Curie conducted pioneering research in radioactivity. Assisted by her husband, Pierre, she discovered two new radioactive elements: polonium and radium. The curie (Ci), a unit of radioactivity, is named for the Curies, as is the chemical element curium.

The youngest of five children, Marie was born on November 7, 1867, to Bronisława and Władysław Skłodowska, both educators. The family lived in the Polish city of Warsaw. During her youth, the family fell on hard times—made worse with the death of Marie's mother in 1878.

A prodigy in literature and math, Marie graduated from high school in 1883. No universities in Poland admitted women, so Marie worked as a governess until 1891, when she spent her savings on a train ticket to Paris and enrolled at the Sorbonne. In 1893, Marie earned a degree in physics and then a degree in mathematics the following year.

Marie met her future husband, Pierre, a physics professor, in 1894. One year later, the pair married in a civil ceremony. The Curies lived modestly, more interested in work than pleasure.

In 1896, Marie learned of Henri Becquerel's observation of radioactivity in uranium. Intrigued, she decided to focus her research on this topic. She soon determined that thorium also displayed radioactivity, and, with Pierre's assistance, she discovered two new radioactive elements: polonium and radium. Marie's research earned her a doctorate degree in 1903—the first woman in France ever to receive one. She also became the first woman ever to win a Nobel Prize—an honor she shared with Becquerel and Pierre in 1903. Curie won a second Nobel Prize in 1911, this one on her own.

Marie and Pierre had two daughters: Irène (1897) and Ève (1904). Although Marie faced tremendous societal pressure to focus on motherhood, she persisted in her work. Perhaps inspired by her mother, Irène became a fine scientist herself, sharing the 1935 Nobel Prize in Chemistry with her husband.

In 1906, Pierre was struck by a horse carriage while crossing the street. He died instantly. Marie coped with this devastating loss by immersing herself even further in her work. She assumed Pierre's professorship at the Sorbonne and, in 1914, expanded her role at the university by opening a radioactivity laboratory, called the Institut du Radium.

During World War I (1914–1918), Marie assisted the Allied war effort by donating two hundred X-ray machines to assist battlefield surgeons. She also outfitted twenty ambulances with portable X-ray machines, often driving these vehicles to the front lines herself.

On July 4, 1934, in the Haute-Savoie region of France, Marie died of leukemia—the result of years of exposure to radioactive material. She was sixty-six years old. Marie is interred in the Panthéon, in Paris, alongside her husband.

SIR J. J. THOMSON (1856–1940)

Sir Joseph John "J. J." Thomson discovered the first subatomic particle (the electron) and formulated the plum pudding model of the atom. He was also an excellent teacher and inspired many of his students to greatness.

Thomson was born on December 18, 1856, near Manchester, England. He was the oldest of two sons born to Emma Thomson, whose family manufactured textiles, and Joseph James Thomson, who sold antique books.

After demonstrating an early aptitude for science, Thomson entered the University of Manchester (then called Owens College), in England, at age fourteen. Afterward, Thomson won a scholarship to the prestigious Trinity College at Cambridge University, also in England. He would remain there—first as a student; then as a professor, researcher, and chair of the Physics Department at the Cavendish Laboratory; and finally, as the headmaster—

for the rest of his life. While at Trinity College, Thomson discovered the electron, which earned him a Nobel Prize in Physics in 1906 and knighthood in 1908.

It was also at Trinity College that Thomson met Rose Paget. Rose's father was a fellow Cambridge professor, and Rose herself was one of Thomson's students. The two married in 1890. They had two children: daughter Joan and son George. George went on to become a notable physicist in his own right, winning the Nobel Prize in Physics in 1937.

Thomson is widely known for his scientific research, but he was also an excellent teacher. Indeed, Thomson's son George once wrote of his father, "his importance in physics depended almost as much on the work he inspired in others as on that which he did himself." No fewer than seven of Thomson's students went on to win the Nobel Prize, including Ernest Rutherford and Niels Bohr. Thomson, said George, "considered teaching to be helpful for a researcher, since it required him to reconsider basic ideas that otherwise might have been taken for granted."

Thomson, a devout Anglican, enjoyed many hobbies, including reading, attending the theater, and cheering on the Cambridge cricket and rugby teams. But, it was botany that really captured his interest. He frequently rambled the countryside outside Cambridge in search of rare specimens for his garden.

Thomson died on August 30, 1940, at the age of eighty-three. He is buried in Westminster Abbey, in London, alongside Sir Isaac Newton and Charles Darwin.

ERNEST LORD RUTHERFORD (1871–1937)

In the early 1900s, Ernest Rutherford conducted important studies on radioactivity. Later in his career, he formulated a new model of the atom, in which electrons orbited around a nucleus inside the atom; discovered the proton; and predicted the existence of the neutron. The rutherford (Rd), which measures radioactive decay, is named for Rutherford, as is the chemical element rutherfordium.

Rutherford was born in rural New Zealand, on August 30, 1871. He was one of twelve children. His father, James, was a farmer. His mother, Martha, taught school. After attending a nearby high school, Rutherford won a scholarship to the University of New Zealand, where he played rugby, participated in the debate society, and studied physics. In 1895, Rutherford won a fellowship to study at the Cavendish Laboratory at Trinity College, in Cambridge, England. J. J. Thomson served as Rutherford's academic advisor, and Rutherford assisted Thomson in his research. Rutherford also conducted his own research in radioactivity.

In 1898, at Thomson's recommendation, Rutherford accepted an academic position at McGill University, in Montreal, Canada. While at McGill, Rutherford continued his research into radioactivity. Working with a scientist named Frederick Soddy, Rutherford observed three types of radioactive decay: alpha decay, beta decay, and gamma decay. He also concluded that radioactive decay occurred in a predictable pattern, called a half-life. For his work in this field, Rutherford won the Nobel Prize for Physics in 1908, was knighted in 1914, and became a lord in 1931.

Rutherford married Mary Georgina Newton, to whom he became engaged before leaving New Zealand, in 1900. The couple had one daughter, named Eileen. In 1907, Rutherford returned to England to become the chair of the Physics Department at the Victoria University of Manchester, in England, where he developed his famous atomic model. World War I forced Rutherford to shift his focus to study the use of sonar in submarines. In 1919, Rutherford returned to the Cavendish Laboratory at Cambridge—this time as its head. He continued his research, however, discovering the proton in 1920 and predicting the existence of the neutron one year later.

Rutherford died on October 19, 1937, of a strangulated hernia. He was sixty-six years old. He is buried at Westminster Abbey near Sir Isaac Newton, Charles Darwin, and his mentor, J. J. Thomson.

NIELS BOHR

Niels Bohr applied the principles of quantum physics to the atom to develop a new atomic model. Bohr also studied radioactivity and predicted the existence of various chemical elements. Bohr was born on October 7, 1885, in Copenhagen, Denmark. His father, Christian, was a university professor. His mother, Ellen, came from a prominent Jewish family. Bohr had an older sister and a younger brother. As a child, Bohr was a talented football (soccer) player, but his future lay in academia.

Bohr commenced his studies at the University of Copenhagen, in 1903. He focused on physics, astronomy,

Niels Bohr applied the theories of quantum physics to develop a new atomic model.

mathematics, and philosophy. He earned his master's degree in 1909 and a doctorate degree in 1911.

In 1916, after holding academic posts at various institutions, Bohr returned to the University of Copenhagen, in Denmark. There, in addition to serving as chair of the Theoretical Physics Department, he founded the Institute of Theoretical Physics, one of the most influential centers of thought on quantum physics in the world. In 1922, Bohr won the Nobel Prize in Physics for his work investigating the structure of atoms and the radiation that emanates from them.

In 1910, Bohr met Margrethe Nørlund. The couple married two years later. The daughter of a pharmacist, Margrethe was instrumental to Bohr's success. As one family friend observed, she had "a decisive role in making his whole scientific and personal activity possible and harmonious." One of the couple's six children (all sons) agreed, noting that "her opinions were his guidelines in daily affairs."

During the early years of the Nazi era in Germany, Bohr offered up the Institute of Theoretical Physics as a safe haven for Jewish scientists fleeing Hitler—at least until 1940, when the Nazis occupied Denmark. In 1943, the Nazis determined that because Bohr's mother had been Jewish, Bohr was too. Bohr and his family fled Denmark, first to Sweden and then to England. Bohr then served alongside several British scientists involved in an American program to research nuclear weapons, called the Manhattan Project. After the war, Bohr became a powerful advocate for international cooperation on nuclear energy.

On November 18, 1962, Bohr died of heart failure in his Copenhagen home. He was seventy-seven years old.

SIR JAMES CHADWICK (1891–1974)

Sir James Chadwick is hailed among scientists for his confirmation of the existence of the neutron. Chadwick was also deeply involved in the Manhattan Project.

The eldest of four children, Chadwick was born on October 20, 1891, in Bollington, England, to John, a cotton spinner, and Anne, a domestic servant. At the age of sixteen, Chadwick won a scholarship to Victoria University of Manchester, in England. Chadwick had planned to study mathematics, but he enrolled in the university's physics program, run by Ernest Rutherford, by accident. Under Rutherford's tutelage, Chadwick earned his bachelor's degree in 1911 and his master's degree in 1913.

In 1913, Chadwick moved to Berlin, Germany, to study radiation under Hans Geiger (1882–1945), the inventor of the Geiger counter, which detects and measures radioactivity. Unfortunately for Chadwick, World War I broke out while he was in Berlin. The Germans detained Chadwick and imprisoned him in an internment camp for the duration of the war.

After the war, Chadwick returned to England to again study under Rutherford—first in Manchester and later at the Cavendish Laboratory at Cambridge University. He earned his PhD in 1921, became a fellow at Gonville and Caius College at Cambridge, and later served as Rutherford's assistant director at the Cavendish Laboratory. It was there

James Chadwick proved the existence of the neutron.

that he proved the existence of the neutron in 1932. For this discovery, Chadwick won the Nobel Prize in Physics in 1935.

Chadwick married Aileen Stewart-Brown, the daughter of a Liverpool stockbroker, in 1925. Two years later the couple welcomed twin girls. Aileen's connection to Liverpool prompted Chadwick to accept the chair of Physics at the University of Liverpool, in England, in 1935, despite the poor condition of the laboratory there. As part of his attempt to modernize the laboratory, Chadwick commissioned the construction of a cyclotron for use in particle experiments.

During World War II (1939–1945), Chadwick worked in the United States as part of the Manhattan Project to build a fission bomb. (Chapter 5 discusses fission bombs in more detail.) His efforts earned him a British knighthood in 1945, but the terrible destruction wrought by the bomb also haunted him for the rest of his life.

In 1948, Chadwick became headmaster of Gonville and Caius College. He remained there until his retirement in 1959. Chadwick died in his sleep on July 24, 1974, in Cambridge. He was eighty-two years old.

OTTO HAHN (1879–1968)

Otto Hahn was a pioneer in the field of radioactivity. In addition to identifying several new radioactive elements, Hahn is credited with the discovery of nuclear fission.

One of four sons, Hahn was born to Charlotte, who was of Jewish ancestry, and Heinrich, a prosperous glazier, on March 8, 1879, in the German city of Frankfurt.

Legendary physicists James Chadwick (*seated, left*), Hans Geiger (*seated, second from left*), Ernest Rutherford (*seated, middle*), and Otto Hahn (*standing, right*), with contemporaries and their wives.

In 1897, Hahn enrolled at the University of Marburg, in Germany, where he received his doctorate in chemistry in 1901. After one year of military service and two years as a lecture assistant at Marburg, Hahn moved to London to study radioactivity at University College. After discovering a new radioactive substance, called radiothorium, Hahn decided to make radioactivity the focus of his research—first at McGill University, in Montreal, Canada, with Ernest Rutherford, and later at the University of Berlin, in Germany.

At the University of Berlin, Hahn met a female scientist named Lise Meitner. The two enjoyed a thirty-year scientific collaboration and a lifelong friendship—but not a romance. In 1911, Hahn met Edith Junghans, an art student, at a conference in Poland. The two married in 1913 and had one son, Hanno, in 1922.

During World War I, Hahn served as a chemical-warfare specialist in the German army. Afterward, he spent several years unraveling the complexities of radioactivity. During the 1930s, Hahn, along with his assistant, Fritz Strassmann and his friend Meitner, produced nuclear fission. For this achievement Hahn (though, curiously, not Meitner or Strassmann) received the 1944 Nobel Prize in Chemistry.

The rise of the Nazis in 1933 placed Hahn in great danger because of his mother's Jewish ancestry. Hahn was unharmed by the murderous regime, however—perhaps because of his scientific expertise. Still, Hahn endured misery of a different sort: continuing his research into nuclear fission, but for the German government, which sought to build a fission bomb.

After the war, the Allies detained several German scientists, including Hahn, in England. During his detention, the Americans dropped two fission bombs in Japan, killing more than two hundred thousand people. Hahn was shattered by this news and even contemplated suicide. After his release in January 1946, Hahn returned to Germany. An outspoken opponent of nuclear weaponry, Hahn served as president of the Kaiser Wilhelm Society (1946–1948) and the Max Planck Society (1948–1960). Hahn died on July 28, 1968, in Göttingen, West Germany. He was eighty-nine years old.

RICHARD FEYNMAN (1918–1988)

Richard Feynman developed the Feynman diagram and united quantum physics with Albert Einstein's theory of special relativity to describe how light and matter interact (called quantum electrodynamics). He also worked on the famous Manhattan Project.

Feynman was born in Queens, New York, on May 11, 1918, to Lucille, a homemaker, and Melville, a salesman. The eldest of three children (one of whom died in infancy), Feynman was slow to speak. However, he demonstrated an early talent for engineering—for example, repairing radios while still in grade school.

After high school, Feynman studied physics at the Massachusetts Institute of Technology, in Cambridge, Massachusetts, earning his bachelor's degree in 1939. He then attended Princeton University, in New Jersey, earning his PhD in 1942.

Feynman married his high-school sweetheart, Arline Greenbaum, in June 1942. Sadly, Arline suffered from tuberculosis and died in 1945. In 1952, Feynman wed Mary Louise Bell, but this marriage ended in divorce in 1958. Feynman married his third wife, an au pair named Gweneth Howarth, in 1960. The couple had one son, Carl (1962), and adopted a daughter, Michelle (1968), and remained together until Feynman's death.

In 1943, the United States government recruited Feynman to work on the top-secret Manhattan Project. The mission of this project was to develop a fission bomb for use in World War II. Feynman accepted the position. Feynman was among the hundreds of scientists who collaborated to successfully design and construct three fission bombs.

In October 1945, Feynman accepted a position at Cornell University, in upstate New York. During his time at Cornell, Feynman developed his now-famous method for expressing the complicated behavior of subatomic particles, called the Feynman diagram.

In 1950, Feynman went to the California Institute of Technology (Caltech), in Pasadena, where he remained for the rest of his career. It was here that Feynman conducted his research on quantum electrodynamics. This work earned Feynman the 1965 Nobel Prize in Physics—an honor he shared with Julian Schwinger (1918–1994) and Shin'ichirō Tomonaga (1906–1979). Feynman died on February 15, 1988, from complications due to a rare form of cancer called liposarcoma. He was sixty-nine years old.

Richared Feynman was part of the Manhattan Project led by Leslie R. Groves (*front, center*). The intense heat of the bomb melted the base of the steel tower on which the first atomic bomb hung when tested near Alamogordo in July 1945.

Standard Model of Elementary Particles

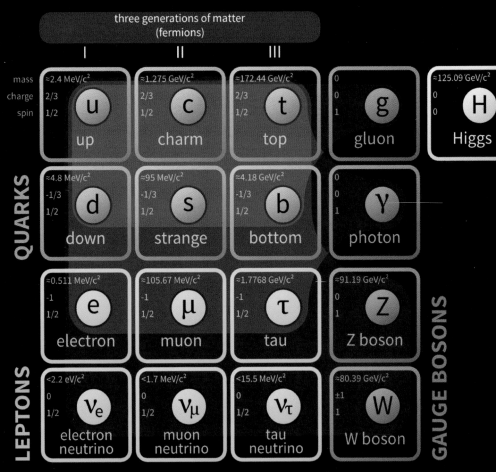

The standard model categorizes elementary particles.

CHAPTER 4

Particle Physics and the Standard Model

A combination of events—most notably Sir J. J. Thomson's 1897 discovery of the electron (the first subatomic particle ever detected), the observation of radiation by Henri Becquerel and Marie and Pierre Curie, and the advent of quantum physics—paved the way for a new form of science, called particle physics. Scientists studying this discipline, also called high-energy physics, would develop a more accurate atomic model that reflects the rules of quantum physics; gain an understanding of the forces (and even identify new forces) that dictate the behavior of subatomic particles; and identify new subatomic particles, including several elementary particles. An elementary particle is a subatomic particle that cannot be broken down any further and that contains no smaller parts inside it.

To keep track of these new elementary particles, particle physicists developed a framework called the standard model. This framework, much like the periodic table for chemical elements developed by Dmitri Mendeleev in 1869, classifies each known elementary particle (including its characteristics and behaviors). The standard model also predicts how these particles interact and describes the fundamental forces behind their behavior. The standard model has helped scientists predict and confirm the existence of several new particles.

CHANGES to the ATOMIC MODEL

As noted in chapter 1, Thomson's model of the atom looked a bit like plum pudding, consisting of a positively charged substance in which negatively charged electrons were embedded. In 1911, Ernest Rutherford challenged this model after conducting an experiment that involved directing a beam of alpha particles onto a sheet of very thin gold foil. According to the plum pudding model, all these particles should have passed directly through the foil. To Rutherford's great surprise, however, the foil deflected the particles. This was, said Rutherford, "quite the most incredible event that has ever happened to me in my life." He continued, "It was almost as incredible as if you fired a fifteen-inch shell at a piece of tissue paper and it came back and hit you."

After much contemplation, Rutherford—inspired in part by research conducted by Japanese scientist Hantaro Nagaoka (1865–1950)—concluded that atoms must contain a minute dense center, which he dubbed the nucleus. This nucleus consumed only a tiny portion of the atom's total size, was high in mass, and carried a positive charge. Rutherford further concluded that electrons, which possessed less mass than the nucleus, orbited around it in a circular manner much the way planets orbit the sun—except in Rutherford's model the distance of each electron's orbital path from the nucleus was arbitrary. The rest of the atom, Rutherford said, was nothing more than empty space.

There was just one problem with Rutherford's model: Physics dictated that as an electron orbited the nucleus, it would release energy. This loss of energy would eventually cause the electron to spiral inward and collapse into the nucleus. Atoms in this model would therefore be extremely unstable—meaning they would quickly decohere.

In 1913, Danish physicist Niels Bohr—a close friend of Rutherford's—solved this problem by applying the principles of quantum physics to the Rutherford model. Bohr theorized that the orbital path of an electron wasn't an arbitrary distance from the nucleus; rather, each electron orbited the nucleus at a specific radius, or energy level. Bohr also posited that electrons could instantaneously jump from one of these distinct orbits to another—called a quantum jump. When a quantum jump occurred, Bohr surmised, the atom would either absorb energy or emit energy (depending on whether the electron jumped outward or inward, respectively). Today we call these various orbits shells. The number of electrons on each shell of an atom helps dictate how the atom behaves.

Not to be outdone, in 1920, Rutherford updated his friend Bohr's model of the atom to include an additional subatomic particle. This particle, which Rutherford called a proton, existed inside the nucleus of the atom and carried a positive charge. He also determined that the number of protons in the nucleus of an atom dictated the chemical element of that atom. For example, hydrogen had one proton, helium had two protons, lithium had three protons, and so on. (Incidentally, this number, called an atom's atomic number, is also used to classify each type of atom in the periodic table. For example, the atomic number for hydrogen is 1, the atomic number for helium is 2, the atomic number for lithium is 3, and so forth.)

In 1932, physicist James Chadwick (1891–1974) discovered a second particle inside the atomic nucleus—or, more precisely, confirmed its existence, as theorized by Rutherford in 1921. This particle, called a neutron, carried no charge. Neutrons help bind protons together. Scientists collectively refer to protons and neutrons as nucleons.

All atoms contain at least one proton. All atoms but hydrogen contain at least one proton and one neutron. In other words, hydrogen contains no neutrons. The nucleus of an atom for a particular chemical element can contain varying numbers of neutrons (or, more generally, different masses). For example, although most carbon atoms contain six neutrons, some contain seven neutrons, and others contain eight. These variant forms of the atom are called isotopes.

QUANTUM TUNNELING

The discovery of the nucleus enabled scientists to identify one mechanism behind radioactive decay, which occurs when an atom breaks down: alpha decay. They concluded that alpha decay occurred when an alpha particle, made up of two protons and two neutrons, inside the nucleus of the atom tunneled through the membrane of the nucleus to break through to the other side. This was puzzling, however. The alpha particle lacks sufficient energy to break through this membrane. So, how did it get through? Scientists concluded this behavior, which they called quantum tunneling, was a natural byproduct of the alpha particle's wave properties.

To understand this, imagine the alpha particle is a ball at the bottom of a mound, and you want to roll it up and over the mound to the other side. According to classical physics, if you lack the strength to roll the ball up and over, it will simply roll back down to you. But in quantum physics a ball has wave properties. So, rather than rolling over the mound (the way a particle might), the ball can clear the mound the way a high-jumper clears a horizontal bar without dislodging it. The high jumper's head (one part of the wave) clears the bar first, followed by her back (another part of the wave) and eventually her feet (yet another part of the wave). In this way, the energy of the high jumper—or the ball or the alpha particle—can be lower than that needed to push through a barrier and yet gradually transfer itself past it.

Radioactive decay is just one example of quantum tunneling in action. Quantum tunneling is also the reason behind such natural phenomena as photosynthesis, DNA mutation, and nuclear fusion.

The FOUR FUNDAMENTAL FORCES

Before they could predict or identify additional subatomic or elementary particles, scientists needed a firm understanding of fields. A field is something that exists at every point in a specific region of space. Scientists believe fields are everywhere. They cover every square millimeter of space in the universe.

There are different types of fields, including matter fields and force fields. As you might guess, matter fields contain matter. Force fields are a bit different, however, because they act on matter. There is also a third kind of field, called a Higgs field, which scientists believe imbues particles with mass.

There are four types of force fields. The first is the gravitational field. According to Einstein's theory of general relativity, this field—more popularly referred to as simply gravity—is what keeps planets in orbit around the sun. Gravity, first correctly described by Sir Isaac Newton during the 1600s, is also what holds planets, stars, and galaxies together. Although gravity is the weakest of the four types of force fields, it is the most pervasive. It also boasts the longest range.

The second type of force field is the electromagnetic field. This was the field detected by Michael Faraday and described mathematically by James Clerk Maxwell, as you might recall from chapter 2. This force field, which is considerably stronger than the gravitational field, is the reason for phenomena like light, heat, electricity, and magnetism. It also binds negatively charged electrons to positively charged atomic nuclei, thereby holding the atoms that contain them together.

The third type of force field is the strong field. Much as the electromagnetic field holds atoms together, the strong field holds together the innards of the nucleus in an atom—its protons and neutrons. By extension, the strong field is responsible for the stability of all matter.

This field—proposed in 1935 by Japanese scientist Hideki Yukawa (1907–1981) and later confirmed by other scientists—is the strongest of all the forces. Indeed, it is as many as one hundred times stronger than the next strongest force, which is electromagnetism. Its range is very short, however.

Finally, the fourth type of force field is the weak field. Like the strong field, the weak field acts inside the nucleus of an atom. But instead of binding its innards together, it triggers a type of radioactive decay called beta decay. In beta decay, a neutron is transformed into a proton (or vice versa), thereby changing the atom containing it into a different chemical element altogether. (This process also results in the release of an electron and of another particle called an antineutrino.) Despite its name, the weak force is not the weakest of the four forces. As mentioned, that honor belongs to gravity. Its range, like that of the strong force, is very short.

In recent years scientists have concluded that the electromagnetic force and the weak force are in fact two facets of a single more fundamental force, which they call the electroweak force. They suspect that the strong force, and perhaps even gravity, is also part of this same force, but they have yet to prove this. The notion that all these forces are in fact facets of one unified force is called the grand unified theory. Another theory, called the theory of everything, goes even further, suggesting that all four forces are facets of one unified force. This theory of everything also brings into alignment Einstein's theory of general relativity and quantum physics, which are currently considered mutually incompatible.

ELEMENTARY PARTICLES

Since the discovery of the electron, scientists have hypothesized or discovered even smaller particles. Some of these are elementary particles—that is, particles that cannot be broken down further and contain no smaller parts inside them.

Elementary particles are small—in fact, they are really small. To get a grasp on just how small these particles are, consider that the typical atom is one ten-billionth of a meter wide. Now consider that an atom's nucleus is just one ten-thousandth the width of an atom; a single nucleon is about one-tenth the width of the nucleus; and a single elementary particle called a quark is less than one one-thousandth the width of a nucleon. (You'll find out more about quarks in the next section.)

Scientists have identified several types of elementary particles, each with its own mass (which may in some cases be zero), charge (positive, negative, or neutral), and spin (angular momentum). Some elementary particles are also differentiated by a characteristic called color. In the "real" world (the one we see), color is a product of visible light on the electromagnetic spectrum. In the quantum world of elementary particles, however, the concept of color is applied differently. Here, color describes a type of charge, similar to electrical charge, rather than a visual phenomenon. There are three color charges: red, green, and blue. Particles with a red charge attract particles with a green charge; particles with a green charge attract particles with a blue charge; and particles with a blue charge attract particles with a red charge. Particles of the same color, in contrast, repel each other. The study of color in particle physics is called quantum chromodynamics.

Elementary particles are categorized into two main groups: fermions and bosons. Fermions, which are named after Italian physicist Enrico Fermi (1901–1954), are generally described as matter particles. This means they serve as the foundation of all matter. In contrast, bosons—named for Indian physicist Satyendra Nath Bose (1894–1974)—are force particles. As such, they mediate interactions among fermions. Each type of boson is associated with a fundamental force— electromagnetic, strong, or weak. Currently, scientists have not discovered a boson associated with gravity, but they postulate that one exists.

In addition to these are a group of particles called antiparticles. Every single type of fermion and boson is associated with an antiparticle, which has the same mass and spin but the opposite charge and color. For example, the antiparticle of an electron is called a positron. When a particle collides with its antiparticle, both particles are annihilated. Fortunately, the universe contains more particles, like electrons, protons, and neutrons, than it does antiparticles like positrons, antiprotons, and antineutrons. Otherwise, the universe and everything in it would be destroyed!

FERMIONS

Fermions come in two varieties. One is called a quark. Scientists have discovered six varieties, or flavors, of quarks. They divide these flavors into two groups based on the direction of their spin. One group, called up-type quarks, consists of up quarks, charm quarks, and top quarks. The other group, called down-type quarks, includes down quarks, strange quarks, and bottom quarks. All six flavors of quarks respond to all four of the fundamental forces: gravity, electromagnetic, strong, and weak.

Up quarks and down quarks, which have the least mass, combine to form the protons and neutrons inside the nucleus of an atom. A proton contains two up quarks and one down quark. A neutron is composed of one up quark and two down quarks. Up and down quarks can also combine with other particles to form compound particles, such as mesons. (Mesons will be discussed momentarily.)

Charm quarks and strange quarks are heavier than up quarks and down quarks—that is, they have more mass. Top quarks and bottom quarks are heavier still. These quarks can combine with up and down quarks and with their own antiparticles to produce a range of particles called hadrons. (Read on to learn more about these.)

The other variety of fermion is called a lepton (from the Greek *leptos*, meaning "small" or "slight"). As with quarks, leptons come in six flavors, only these flavors relate not to spin but to electrical charge. Leptons possessing an electrical charge include electrons, muons, and taus. (For all three, this electrical charge is negative.) Neutral leptons have no electrical charge. Collectively called neutrinos, these neutral leptons consist of electron-neutrinos, muon-neutrinos, and tau-neutrinos.

Charged leptons react to gravity, electromagnetism, and the weak force, but not the strong force. The lightest of the charged leptons, electrons, are the driving force behind both chemical bonding and chemical reactions—and hence all life. They are stable particles, meaning they don't tend to decohere or decay. Muons, which are heavier than electrons but lighter than protons, are significantly less stable than electrons, with a lifespan of 2.2 millionths of a second, after which they decay into other particles. Taus are even heavier and more unstable, decaying after just 2.9 ten-trillionths of a second.

Neutrinos, which, as mentioned, have no electric charge, are different. They have virtually no mass and are influenced only by nature's two weakest forces: gravity and the weak force. For this reason, neutrinos barely react to matter. Indeed, they pass right through it at nearly the speed of light, which makes them difficult to detect and measure. Neutrinos can change from electron-neutrinos to muon-neutrinos to tau-neutrinos and back again, but there appears to be little difference between them. This behavior is called oscillation.

GHOST PARTICLES

In 1930, a scientist named Wolfgang Pauli predicted the existence of neutrinos when an equation he was formulating just wouldn't add up. "I have done something very bad today by proposing a particle that cannot be detected," Pauli wrote in his journal. "It is something no theorist should ever do."

Since then, scientists have detected neutrinos (often called ghost particles), and they know these particles exist in vast numbers. Indeed, scientists postulate as many as one hundred trillion neutrinos pass through us every second!

Scientists also know where neutrinos originate. They originate from explosions like the big bang and from stars like our sun.

As for the role of neutrinos in the ecosystem that is our universe, scientists remain unsure, but they suspect it may have something to do with why the universe contains significantly more matter than antimatter and, by extension, why anything exists at all. (Antimatter is formed by atoms consisting of antiparticles rather than standard particles.)

BOSONS

As mentioned, bosons are force particles (sometimes called messenger particles) that mediate interactions among fermions. Bosons are associated with three of the four fundamental forces: electromagnetic, strong, and weak. (Again, scientists have yet to discover a boson associated with gravity.) If fermions are the building block of matter, bosons are a little like the mortar that holds them together.

As with fermions, there are two types of bosons: gauge bosons and scalar bosons. The gauge boson associated with the electromagnetic force is called a photon. The photon, which possesses zero mass but exhibits characteristics like energy, momentum, and spin, enables electrically charged particles such as electrons and protons to interact with each other. Photons themselves, however, possess no electrical or color charge. This means that the electromagnetic field does not influence their behavior, and they cannot directly interact with each other.

A gauge boson, called a gluon, is associated with the strong force. They act as the "glue" that holds quarks inside

Peter Higgs theorized the existence of the Higgs boson.

protons and other particles (hence their name). From a physical standpoint, gluons are much like photons, with one exception: they possess a color charge. As a result, they can interact with each other and limit each other's range. This is the mechanism behind the strong force.

The weak force is associated with not one but three gauge bosons: the W+ boson, the W- boson, and the Z boson. The W bosons, as they're often called, are massive particles—eighty times heavier than a proton. The two varieties of W bosons, which possess opposite electrical charges and serve as each other's antiparticle, play a key role in beta decay. The Z boson is even more massive than the W boson, but it has zero charge. Z bosons can alter the spin, momentum, and energy of other particles. All three of these particles experience very brief lifespans—even shorter than that of a tau.

So far scientists have detected just one type of scalar boson: the Higgs boson. In 1960, a scientist named Peter Higgs (1929–) predicted the existence of this boson; in 2012, it was actually detected. The Higgs boson exhibits zero spin, zero electrical charge, and zero color charge, and it decays almost immediately. The Higgs boson is associated with the Higgs field, which, as mentioned, scientists believe imbues particles with mass.

It's impossible to overstate the significance of the discovery of the Higgs boson. Indeed, for many physicists, it's the final piece of the puzzle that represents our current grasp of our universe. Scientists believe that without the Higgs boson there could be no atoms; thus, there could be no life. This explains why some call this boson the "God particle."

FEYNMAN DIAGRAMS

In working to discover these different particles, scientists rely on mathematical tools. Mathematics can advance science

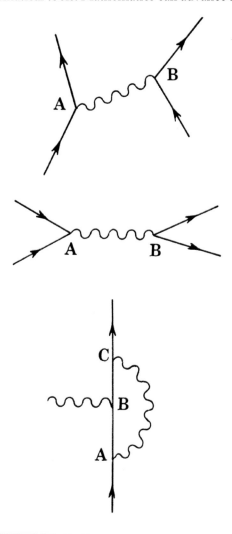

Feynman diagrams help scientists describe and visualize the behavior of particles.

by making sense of data. But the math required to describe the behavior of subatomic particles, such as their paths and trajectories, is quite complex. To help scientists describe and visualize this behavior more easily, American physicist Richard Feynman developed a system to diagram them.

In these diagrams, called Feynman diagrams, the vertical axis represents time and the horizontal one represents space. Fermions are depicted with straight lines, with arrows to indicate their direction of movement, and bosons appear as wavy ones. A vertex is used to show when a particle interacts with another particle or with a force (such as the electromagnetic force, the strong force, or the weak force). Lines whose arrow points toward a vertex represent the "past," while lines whose arrows point away from it represent the "future" or final state.

COMPOUND PARTICLES

Both fermions and bosons can combine to form compound particles. Examples of compound particles include baryons (made of three quarks) and mesons (composed of one quark and one antiquark), both of which are also called hadrons. Other examples include positroniums (made of an electron and a positron); protons and neutrons (also made of three quarks); and even whole atoms. Compound particles can behave like fermions or bosons, depending on their composition. Like elementary particles, these compound particles are also associated with antiparticles. Using a special machine called a particle collider, scientists have discovered more than two hundred of these compound

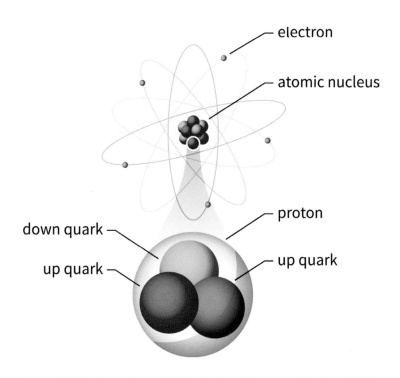

electron

atomic nucleus

proton

down quark

up quark

up quark

A proton consists of two up quarks and a down quark.

particles—most of them highly unstable with extremely short lifespans.

HYPOTHETICAL PARTICLES

Based on observations of known particles, gaps in the standard model, and stubborn equations that just won't solve, scientists have hypothesized the existence of several more particles. The study of hypothetical particles is one branch of a scientific discipline called theoretical particle physics.

One example of a hypothetical particle is a boson called a graviton, which scientists believe is a massless particle associated with the gravitational force. Another example of a hypothetical particle is a leptoquark, which scientists suggest carries information between certain quarks and leptons. There are many more.

During the 1970s, scientists developed a theory called supersymmetry, which dictates that each fermion and boson has what they call a "super partner" of the opposite type. In other words, the super partner of a boson would be a fermion, and the super partner of a fermion would be a boson. If this turns out to be the case, the number of known elementary particles will effectively double!

Particle Colliders

The overlay on this aerial view of CERN and the surrounding region shows the location of the LHC.

A particle collider is a machine that produces collisions between subatomic particles. It consists of a large circular tunnel (usually underground) containing mechanisms that were first called cyclotrons but later renamed particle accelerators. Particle accelerators use electromagnetic fields and radiofrequency cavities to launch charged subatomic particles through the tunnel at enormous speeds. Powerful magnets focus or steer the particle beams. These particles can then be used for a variety of research purposes.

When these particles meet other particles in the tunnel, the resulting collisions release sufficient energy to enable scientists to confirm (or not) the existence of theoretical subatomic particles. It also allows them to predict the existence of completely new particles.

The first particle collider was built in 1932 by Ernest Lawrence (1901–1958) at the University of California, Berkeley. Today there are several particle colliders all over the world, including Brookhaven National Laboratory, the Fermi National Accelerator Laboratory, and the SLAC National Accelerator Laboratory (originally named Stanford Linear Accelerator Center) in the United States; the Budker Institute of Nuclear Physics in Russia; the Deutsches Elektronen-Synchrotron in Germany; the Institute of High Energy Physics in China; and KEK in Japan.

Perhaps the most famous collider is called the Large Hadron Collider (LHC), managed by the European Organization for Nuclear Research (CERN). Opened in 2008, the LHC is the largest and most powerful particle collider in the world. The LHC's tunnel is 17 miles (27 kilometers) around. It was at the LHC that scientists discovered the Higgs boson.

Experts describe the LHC, which employs thousands of physicists from all over the world, as the most complex contraption ever constructed. Indeed, the Large Hadron Collider generates enough data per second to fill more than a thousand one-terabyte hard drives. The LHC lies under the French-Swiss border, near Geneva, Switzerland.

Particle physics has helped scientists better understand the big bang.

CHAPTER 5

The Impact of Particle Physics

Although particle physics and the standard model involve the study of matter on a miniscule scale, their impact has been enormous. One major impact of particle physics and the standard model has been their contribution to our growing understanding of the nature of our universe and how it was formed—in other words, the big bang. But that's not the only impact. Advancements in particle physics have also led to the development of revolutionary technologies that touch every aspect of our lives.

Some of these technologies—such as nuclear energy and weaponry—stem from the direct manipulation of subatomic particles. Others have evolved from tools developed for the study of particle physics. These include medical imaging technologies and technologies for delivering medical treatments and developing new drugs, both of which derive from the powerful particle accelerators used in particle colliders like the Large Hadron Collider. These machines operate by way of a phenomenon called superconductivity, which is also a product of research in particle physics.

PARTICLE PHYSICS and the BIG BANG

The Greek scholar Aristotle believed matter—and, by extension, our universe—was eternal. In other words, the universe was static. It had always existed in its current form, and in that form it would remain.

This view of the universe as a static entity prevailed until the 1920s, when scientists observed that, in fact, the universe appeared to be expanding. (Scientists have since concluded that not only is the universe expanding, but the rate of this expansion has accelerated over time.) In 1927, this discovery led Belgian scientist Georges Lemaître (1894–1966), who was also a monsignor in the Roman Catholic Church, to conclude that the universe must have been smaller in the past. In fact, he suggested, at some moment in the very distant past, the universe, and all the matter it contained, must have been small enough to fit into a single point, which Lemaître called the primordial atom. Finally, Lemaître concluded that something caused this dense primordial atom to explode in a spectacular manner. He believed this explosion must have generated enormous amounts of energy, which flung matter inside the primordial atom ever-outward, resulting in the formation of our universe. Although the scientific community initially viewed Lemaître's hypothesis—later named the big bang—with great skepticism, it has since become the generally accepted explanation for the origin of our universe.

Today's particle colliders simulate the conditions of the big bang by using particle accelerators to propel particles at incredible speeds to produce collisions that generate enormous amounts of energy. As mentioned, this technology has helped particle physicists predict the existence of and identify new particles. But it has also helped them to gain important insight into the birth of our universe and perhaps into how it might change in the future.

Thanks in part to these insights, scientists have estimated that the big bang occurred roughly 13.8 billion years ago. They calculate that within its first second of existence, the universe contained the four fundamental forces, elementary particles like fermions and leptons (and their antiparticles), and nucleons like protons and neutrons. Within three minutes, powerful collisions between protons and neutrons produced trace amounts of the chemical elements lithium, hydrogen (in isotope form), and helium. However, it would be hundreds of millions of years before conditions arose that allowed for the formation of galaxies, stars, and planets. It would be about nine billion years before our own solar system formed.

NUCLEAR ENERGY and WEAPONRY

Most scientists contend that nuclear power is a safe and sustainable energy source that produces virtually no air pollution. However, many people oppose its use, claiming it poses a threat to the health of humans and the environment. To support these claims, antinuclear activists cite nuclear accidents, such as those at Three Mile Island (1979), Chernobyl (1986), and Fukushima (2011), as well as the radioactive nuclear waste produced by the fission process. But, what exactly is the fission process, and how is nuclear

Limitations of the Standard Model

The standard model is an effective framework for classifying known elementary particles, predicting how they interact, and describing the fundamental forces involved in their behavior. But it doesn't explain everything. "The universe," says contemporary particle physicist Hitoshi Murayama, "is a deeper puzzle than the standard model." In a sense, the model cannot keep up with new discoveries that are made.

For example, the standard model accommodates only three of the four fundamental forces— electromagnetic, strong, and weak. It has yet to identify how gravity fits in the picture. (However, as mentioned, it does leave room for the discovery of a new boson called a graviton. The graviton is the particle that is thought to be the carrier of the gravitational field.)

The standard model also fails to accommodate a hypothetical type of matter called dark matter or a hypothetical type of energy called dark energy. The Swiss astronomer Fritz Zwicky first used the term "dark matter" in the 1930s. Scientists describe dark matter as weakly interactive massive particles, or WIMPs.

They believe WIMPs, which interact only through gravity and the weak force, comprise nearly 85 percent of all mass in the universe. As for dark energy, scientists believe it is the force behind the universe's accelerated expansion.

The standard model holds that neutrinos lack mass. However, scientists have conducted experiments that seem to suggest otherwise. This represents another lapse in the standard model. Finally, the standard model does not explain why the universe contains so much more matter than antimatter.

Perhaps as scientists make more discoveries in particle physics, they will be able to adapt the standard model to accommodate these lapses.

energy created? Let's explore how the fission process was discovered and the other applications for this discovery.

Around the turn of the twentieth century, scientists like Henri Becquerel, Marie Curie, Pierre Curie, and Ernest Rutherford made important discoveries relating to radioactive decay—specifically, atoms of radioactive elements, such as uranium, polonium, and radium, naturally transmuted into atoms of other elements.

In 1917, Ernest Rutherford proved it was possible to induce transmutation in the lab by bombarding nitrogen atoms with alpha particles to produce oxygen. During the late 1930s, Otto Hahn, Lise Meitner (1878–1968), and Fritz Strassmann (1902–1980) conducted similar studies—except they bombarded uranium atoms with neutrons. However, this operation did more than simply transmute one element into another (in this case, uranium into barium and krypton). It also freed numerous particles from the nucleus, including neutrons, and released significant amounts of energy. This process became known as nuclear fission.

In 1939, Hungarian physicist Leó Szilárd (1898–1964) hypothesized that nuclear fission could unleash a chain reaction. In other words, a fission reaction in one uranium atom could emit a neutron that could then collide with another uranium atom to trigger a new fission reaction. Moreover, if that first uranium atom released more than one neutron, the number of ensuing fission reactions could grow exponentially, releasing enormous amounts of energy. Two other scientists, Irène Joliot-Curie (1897–1956) and Frédéric Joliot-Curie (1900–1958), came to the same conclusion at around the same time. In December 1942, Italian scientist Enrico Fermi confirmed the hypothesis put forth by Szilárd and the Joliot-Curies by constructing a machine that successfully triggered this nuclear chain reaction. Fermi's machine, which he called an atomic pile, was the first operational nuclear reactor.

Szilárd envisioned the nuclear chain reaction as a means by which to generate clean and sustainable electric power to illuminate entire cities, drive production in factories, and more. Over the next several decades, Szilárd's vision was realized as countries all over the world constructed nuclear power plants. Today, there are nearly 450 of these plants, which generate roughly 11 percent of the world's electricity.

Szilárd also grasped, however, that the nuclear chain reaction could conceivably be used to produce bombs of unparalleled destructive force. He wasn't the only one. In April 1939, scientists in Germany launched an effort to build just such a bomb to gain an advantage against the Allies in World War II, and scientists in America weren't far behind. In August 1945, the United States won the race to develop the fission bomb, detonating two of them over the Japanese cities of Hiroshima and Nagasaki to hasten Japan's surrender in World War II.

These bombs caused unparalleled death and destruction. The blast in Hiroshima vaporized more than 4.7 square miles (12 square kilometers) of the city and destroyed almost 70 percent of its buildings. Tens of thousands of the city's inhabitants, most of them civilians, died instantly— some simply vanishing in the intense heat produced by the explosion. Thousands more perished in the white-hot fires that swept the city in the aftermath of the explosion or from the long-term effects of radiation exposure. The bombing of Nagasaki produced similar results (albeit on a smaller scale).

This mushroom cloud hovered over Nagasaki after the atomic bombing on August 9, 1945.

Experts estimate that together these bombs killed more than two hundred thousand people—more than a third of the total population of both cities combined. Although the United States' bombings of Hiroshima and Nagasaki were the first and only nuclear attacks in history, the threat of nuclear war looms large even today.

NUCLEAR FUSION

Nuclear fission isn't the only source of nuclear energy or weaponry. Another source is nuclear fusion. Nuclear fusion occurs when two nuclei with low mass, such as the nuclei in hydrogen atoms, move so close together that the strong force acting inside them fuses them together. The result is the formation of a single atom and the release of enormous amounts of energy.

Nuclear fusion occurs only when certain environmental conditions are met. First, the temperature must be extremely high: 100,000,000 Kelvin (180,000,000° Fahrenheit/100,000,000° Celsius). Second, the pressure must be extremely high, causing the atoms to be squeezed tightly together.

Scientists have sought ways to harness nuclear fusion, which is the process that powers stars like our sun, to produce clean power or for use in weapons (called thermonuclear weapons). So far, they have been unable to induce nuclear fusion on its own. However, they have induced nuclear fusion by first inducing a fission reaction to generate the necessary temperature and pressure.

SUPERCONDUCTIVITY

As discussed, by the late 1800s, scientists had developed an excellent understanding of how electricity behaved. They knew electrical charges could move to create a current. They knew a current could follow a particular path, called a circuit. Finally, they knew that current flowed, or conducted, better through some materials (called conductors) than others (called insulators). This blockage of current, called resistance, was a bit like an electrical version of friction.

Scientists had not, however, determined the mechanisms behind current, conduction, and resistance. That would wait until Sir J. J. Thomson's discovery of the electron in 1897. Armed with this discovery, scientists made the following conclusions: the electrical charges that moved to form a current were in fact electrons, conduction occurred when a material released its own electrons into the current, and resistance occurred when a material did not release its electrons.

In 1911, while studying the properties of a chemical element called mercury, Dutch physicist Heike Kamerlingh Onnes (1853–1926) discovered that when it plunged below a critical temperature of 4.2 Kelvin (−452.11° Fahrenheit/−268.95° Celsius), its electrical resistance fell to zero. In other words, an electrical current could pass through the mercury unimpeded, and if the mercury were formed into a loop, the current would flow forever. This was a shocking discovery. Scientists had never observed such behavior in even the most efficient conductors.

Scientists called this phenomenon superconductivity. The materials that exhibited it were called superconductors,

THEORY OF
SUPERCONDUCTIVITY

THEORETICAL PHYSICIST JOHN BARDEEN WAS THE FIRST
PERSON TO WIN TWO NOBEL PRIZES IN THE SAME FIELD.
HIS FIRST, IN 1956, SHARED WITH WALTER BRATTAIN
AND WILLIAM SHOCKLEY, WAS FOR THE INVENTION OF
THE TRANSISTOR, THE BASIC COMPONENT OF ELEC-
TRONIC INFORMATION TECHNOLOGIES. HIS SECOND,
HERE AT THE UNIVERSITY OF ILLINOIS IN 1972, SHARED
WITH POSTDOCTORAL ASSOCIATE LEON N. COOPER
AND GRADUATE STUDENT J. ROBERT SCHRIEFFER, WAS
FOR THE EXPLANATION OF SUPERCONDUCTIVITY, A
STATE OF MATTER FIRST OBSERVED IN 1911 IN WHICH
MATERIALS LOSE THEIR ELECTRICAL RESISTANCE AT
LOW TEMPERATURES. THE BCS THEORY, ANNOUNCED IN
1957 AND BASED ON A MODEL IN WHICH ELECTRONS
FORM BOUND PAIRS, EXPLAINS FUNDAMENTAL PROC-
ESSES IN SOLID-STATE PHYSICS, NUCLEAR PHYSICS,
ASTROPHYSICS AND PARTICLE PHYSICS.

UNIVERSITY OF ILLINOIS

This plaque at the University of Illinois
Urbana-Champaign commemorates the theory of
superconductivity developed by John Bardeen and
his students.

which we now know include thirty pure metals, numerous
alloys, and certain ceramics, each with its own critical
temperature. Soon scientists found that superconductors
exhibited another interesting characteristic: they were
unaffected by magnetic fields (provided the field was
sufficiently weak).

Although superconductivity was first observed in
1911, the mechanism behind it remained an enigma
until 1957, when three American scientists named John
Bardeen (1908–1991), Leon N. Cooper (1930–), and John R.
Schrieffer (1931–) published a theory called the Bardeen-
Cooper-Schrieffer (BCS) theory. This theory explained both

characteristics of superconductors: their lack of electrical resistance and their lack of response to weak magnetic fields.

The BCS theory states that when a material reaches its critical temperature, all its electrons group themselves into pairs, called Cooper pairs. All these Cooper pairs then join to create one single organized entity that forms a current. Because none of the atoms in the superconducting material retain their electrons, they produce no resistance, so the current continues indefinitely or until the material is sufficiently warmed to raise it above its critical temperature. Because the energy needed to disrupt the current equates more closely to the energy needed to break up all the Cooper pairs than to the energy needed to break up a single pair, weaker magnetic fields do not disturb the material.

The discovery of superconductivity heralded the development of myriad machines, including powerful particle accelerators and medical devices. Similar to superconductivity is superfluidity. Superfluidity describes a liquid or fluid that possesses zero viscosity or friction. In other words, when a superfluid flows, it loses no energy. This phenomenon was first explained by Richard Feynman.

MEDICAL APPLICATIONS

Doctors use medical imaging technologies such as magnetic resonance imaging (MRI) and positron emission topography (PET) to diagnose disease in patients. Both these machines descended from the particle accelerator, which particle physicists developed to detect and observe subatomic particles.

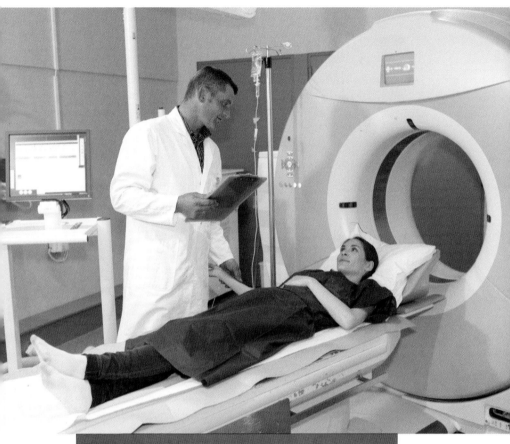

The magnetic resonance imaging (MRI) machine descends from the particle accelerator.

Machines derived from particle accelerators also play a role in the treatment of certain medical conditions such as cancer. One such treatment is called proton beam therapy (PBT). PBT, a type of radiation therapy, uses a small particle accelerator to blast cancerous tumors with a precise and powerful beam of protons.

The proton beam damages the tumor's DNA, which either kills the tumor's cells or prevents the cells from reproducing. One advantage of this treatment technique is that it causes minimal damage to healthy tissue surrounding the tumor.

Doctors also use machines derived from particle accelerators in another type of cancer treatment: neutron capture therapy (NCT). NCT involves a two-step process: First, doctors inject the tumor with a chemical element called boron. Then, they use a small particle accelerator to blast the tumor with a beam of high-energy neutrons. The neutrons are absorbed by the injected boron, which then emits high-energy charged particles that kill the surrounding cancer cells.

NCT is often used in the treatment of head and neck cancers. PBT and NCT are just two examples of cancer treatments that involve the use of a particle accelerator.

Special particle accelerators called synchrotrons serve another medical purpose: to develop pharmaceuticals. These machines work by blasting a virus with powerful X-ray beams made of photons to reveal its precise physical structure.

This information enables researchers to identify potential drug candidates to counteract the virus. Researchers used this method to develop Kaletra, which combats the AIDS virus, and Tamiflu, which helps slow the spread of influenza.

Scientists have also begun using synchrotrons to investigate the cause of such diseases as diabetes, Alzheimer disease, and amyotrophic lateral sclerosis (ALS). Indeed, Nobel laureate Roger Kornberg, who heads a research lab at Stanford Medical School, in California, believes "the whole future of drug development lies in synchrotrons."

The discovery of subatomic particles, starting with the electron, combined with a growing understanding of quantum physics, yielded an entirely new field of scientific study: particle physics. Particle physicists study the tiniest of particles, but their research has enormous implications. It has changed our understanding of our universe and resulted in the development of life-saving technologies. No doubt future discoveries in particle physics—whether they relate to the detection of the graviton or some other particle, the true nature of dark matter and dark energy, or something scientists haven't even conceived of yet—will prove just as profound!

Chronology

400 BCE

Leucippus and Democritus propose that matter is made of *a-tomos*. Empedocles posits that all matter is made of earth, water, air, and fire.

300 BCE

Aristotle adds a fifth element to Empedocles's list: aether.

700 CE Abu Mūsā Jābir ibn Hayyān adds two philosophical elements to Aristotle's model: sulfur and mercury.

1661 Robert Boyle publishes *The Sceptical Chymist,* which posits that matter is made of tiny particles that move and clump together to form masses that are difficult to divide.

1669 For the first time, a scientist, named Hennig Brand, discovers a new chemical element in a laboratory rather than in nature.

1704   Sir Isaac Newton publishes *Opticks: or, A treatise of the reflexions, refractions, inflexions and colours of light*. Also two treatises of the species and magnitude of curvilinear figures. His text proposes that matter is made of corpuscles.

1714   Gottfried Leibniz proposes an alternative to the corpuscle: the monad.

1758   Ruđer Bošković formulates a new atomic model consisting of atom points surrounded by fields with positive and negative charges.

1803   John Dalton produces the atomic model that is the basis of our modern model.

1811   Amedeo Avogadro conceives of the molecule.

1832   Michael Faraday develops the concept of a field.

1869   Dmitri Mendeleev publishes the first periodic table of elements.

1896   Henri Becquerel observes radioactive behavior in uranium.

1897   J. J. Thomson discovers the first subatomic particle: the electron.

1900   Max Planck discovers quantum physics.

1904   Marie Curie proposes that radioactive behavior is a property of certain elements and not the result of some outside stimulus.

1907   Fredrick Soddy and Ernest Rutherford conclude that radioactive behavior is a result of a process called radioactive decay, which occurs over a predictable period.

1911   Ernest Rutherford, inspired in part by Hantaro Nagaoka, concludes that all atoms contain a nucleus. Heike Kamerlingh Onnes discovers superconductivity.

1913   Niels Bohr develops a new atomic model based on the laws of quantum physics.

1920   Ernest Rutherford discovers the proton.

1927   Georges Lemaître proposes that the birth of the universe followed an enormous explosion (now called the big bang) and that the universe is expanding.

1932 James Chadwick discovers the neutron. Ernest Lawrence builds the first particle collider at the University of California, Berkeley.

1939 President Franklin D. Roosevelt spearheads the creation of the Manhattan Project.

1942 Enrico Fermi constructs the first nuclear reactor.

1945 The United States completes the construction of three nuclear bombs and drops two over Japan.

1957 John Bardeen, Leon N. Cooper, and John R. Schrieffer publish the Bardeen-Cooper-Schrieffer (BCS) theory, which explains the mechanism behind superconductivity.

2008 CERN, the European Organization for Nuclear Research, unveils the largest and most powerful particle collider ever built, called the Large Hadron Collider (LHC).

2012 Scientists at CERN discover the Higgs boson.

Glossary

alchemy A forerunner to chemistry whose focus was the discovery of the philosopher's stone, which was said to transform base metals into noble metals like gold and to confer immortality.

allotrope A variant form of a chemical element or molecular substance. For example, a diamond is an allotrope of carbon.

antiparticle A particle with the same mass and spin but opposite charge and color of a fermion, boson, or other particle.

atom The smallest unit of matter that possesses all the properties of a given chemical element.

atomism The theory that matter is composed of atoms.

baryon A compound particle made of three quarks.

boson An elementary particle that mediates interactions among fermions.

chemistry The study of the composition, structure, and properties of substances and of the transformations these substances undergo.

compound particle A particle made of two or more elementary particles.

electron A negatively charged particle that orbits the nucleus of an atom.

elementary particle A subatomic particle that cannot be broken down any further and that contains no smaller parts inside it.

fermion An elementary particle that serves as the foundation of all matter.

field Something that exists at every point in a specific region of space.

fundamental force A force that acts on matter. There are four fundamental forces: the gravitational force, the electromagnetic force, the strong force, and the weak force.

gluon A type of boson associated with the strong force.

graviton A hypothetical particle associated with gravity.

hadron A type of compound particle. Examples of hadrons include baryons and mesons.

half-life The predictable rate of radioactive decay.

isomer A molecule that contains the exact same atoms as a "standard" molecule but in a different arrangement.

isotope A variant form of an atom that contains a different number of neutrons from the "standard" variant.

lepton A type of fermion that is defined by its electrical charge (or lack thereof).

Manhattan Project The United States' effort to develop a fission bomb during World War II.

matter A physical substance that occupies space and possesses mass.

metallurgy The practice of applying heat to manipulate metal.

molecule A group of atoms bound together.

neutrino A type of lepton that possesses no electrical charge.

neutron A subatomic particle that carries no charge and is found inside the nucleus of an atom.

nuclear fission A reaction that occurs when neutrons bombard an atom of uranium and split its nucleus in half and release its contents. The result is the creation of a barium atom and a krypton atom and the release of significant amounts of energy.

nucleus A collection of protons and neutrons packed densely together in the center of an atom. Nuclei possess a positive charge.

particle collider A machine that produces high-speed collisions between subatomic particles.

particle physics The study of subatomic particles and the forces that act on them.

photon A type of boson associated with the electromagnetic force.

quantum physics The study of the nature and behavior of quanta.

quark A type of fermion that is defined by its spin.

radioactive decay Describes when an atom breaks down and transmutes into an atom of a different element.

radioactivity Describes the emission of energy by an atom all by itself rather than in response to some outside stimulus such as the application of heat.

scientific method The methodology scientists use to draw scientific conclusions.

standard model A framework used by particle physicists to classify known elementary particles (including their characteristics and behaviors), predict how they interact, and describe the fundamental forces behind their behavior.

subatomic particle A particle, such as a proton, neutron, or electron, that exists inside an atom.

superconductivity Describes a substance that, when sufficiently cooled, produces zero electrical resistance and is unaffected by weak magnetic fields.

BOOKS

Baxter, Roberta. *The Particle Model of Matter*. Oxford, UK: Raintree, 2009.

Carroll, Sean. *The Particle at the End of the Universe: How the Hunt for the Higgs Boson Leads Us to the Edge of a New World*. New York: Dutton, 2013.

Latta, Sara L. *Smash! Exploring the Mysteries of the Universe with the Large Hadron Collider*. New York: Graphic Universe, 2017.

Morton, Alan. *Splitting the Atom*. New York: Gareth Stevens Publishing, 2005.

Whyntie, Tom, and Oliver Pugh. *Particle Physics: A Graphic Guide*. London: Icon Books, Ltd., 2014.

WEBSITES

The ABCs of Particle Physics

https://www.symmetrymagazine.org/particle-physics-abcs

This engaging website from the United States Department of Energy covers key concepts in particle physics from A to Z.

CERN

https://home.cern/about

Students can learn more about particle physics and CERN's accelerators and experiments through this website. The CERN website also gives updated information on current topics related to particle physics.

The Particle Adventure

http://www.particleadventure.org

This award-winning website from the Particle Data Group at the Lawrence Berkeley National Laboratory offers an interactive guide to elementary particles, dark matter, and more.

Quarked!

http://www.quarked.org

This website breaks down particle physics in language even young children can understand.

Bibliography

Bagley, Mary. "Matter: Definition and the Five States of Matter." Live Science, April 11, 2016. https://www.livescience.com/46506-states-of-matter.html.

"Benefits of Particle Physics." Fermi Research Alliance, LLC. February 9, 2016. http://www.fnal.gov/pub/science/particle-physics/benefits/index.html.

Boyle, Robert. *The Sceptical Chymist: The Classic 1661 Text.* Mineola, NY: Dover Publications, Inc., 2003.

Choi, Charles Q. "Our Expanding Universe: Age, History & Other Facts." Space.com, June 16, 2017. https://www.space.com/52-the-expanding-universe-from-the-big-bang-to-today.html.

Clements, Elizabeth. "Particle Physics Benefits: Adding It Up." *Symmetry*, December 1, 2008. https://www.symmetrymagazine.org/article/december-2008/particle-physics-benefits-adding-it-up.

Curie, Marie. "Radium and Radioactivity." *Century*, January 1904. http://cwp.library.ucla.edu/articles/curie.htm.

Des Jardins, Julie. "Madame Curie's Passion." *Smithsonian*, October 2011. https://www.smithsonianmag.com/history/madame-curies-passion-74183598.

The Editors of Encyclopaedia Britannica. "Particle Physics." Britannica, March 17, 2009. https://www.britannica.com/science/particle-physics.

————. "Quark." Britannica, January 25, 2018. https://www.britannica.com/science/quark.

————. "Weakly Interacting Massive Particle." Britannica, March 9, 2009. https://www.britannica.com/science/weakly-interacting-massive-particle.

Finkbeiner, Ann. "Looking for Neutrinos, Nature's Ghost Particles." *Smithsonian*, November 2010. https://www.smithsonianmag.com/science-nature/looking-for-neutrinos-natures-ghost-particles-64200742.

Freed, Fred, dir. "The Decision to Drop the Bomb." NBC White Paper, 1965.

Gerbis, Nicholas. "What Is Superconductivity?" How
    Stuff Works. Accessed March 5, 2018. https://
    science.howstuffworks.com/environmental/energy/
    superconductivity.htm.

Leibniz, G. W. *The Principles of Philosophy Known as
    Monadology*. Translated by Robert Latta. Oxford, UK:
    The Clarendon Press, 1898.

Mastin, Luke. "Timeline of the Big Bang." Physics of
    the Universe. Accessed March 5, 2018. http://www.
    physicsoftheuniverse.com/topics_bigbang_timeline.html.

Mead, George Robert Stow. *Thrice-Greatest Hermes:
    Excerpts and Fragments*. London: Theosophical
    Publishing Society, 1906.

Newton, Isaac. *Opticks: or, A treatise of the reflections,
    refractions, inflexions and colours of light. Also two
    treatises of the species and magnitude of curvilinear figures*.
    London: William and John Innys at the West End of St.
    Paul's, 1730.

"Superconductivity." CERN. Accessed March 5, 2018.
    https://home.cern/about/engineering/superconductivity.

Sutton, Christine. "Gluon." Britannica, July 20, 1998.
    https://www.britannica.com/science/gluon.

————. "Higgs Boson." Britannica, July 5, 2012. https://www.britannica.com/science/Higgs-boson.

————. "Quantum Chromodynamics." Britannica, July 20, 2006. https://www.britannica.com/science/quantum-chromodynamics.

————. "Subatomic Particle." Britannica, March 16, 2007. https://www.britannica.com/science/particle-physics.

Thomson, George Paget. "J. J. Thomson." Britannica, July 20, 1998. https://www.britannica.com/biography/J-J-Thomson.

Thomson, J. J. "Cathode Rays." *Philos. Mag.* 44 (1897): 293.

Tuttle, Kelen. "Why Particle Physics Matters." *Symmetry*, October 29, 2013. https://www.symmetrymagazine.org/article/october-2013/why-particle-physics-matters.

White, Lori Ann. "Shedding Light." *Symmetry*, May 1, 2011. https://www.symmetrymagazine.org/article/may-2011/shedding-light.

Williams, L. Pearce. "Michael Faraday: British Physicist and Chemist." Britannica, July 26, 1999. https://www.britannica.com/biography/Michael-Faraday.

Index

About the Author

Kate Shoup has written more than forty books and has edited hundreds more. When not working, Shoup loves to travel, watch IndyCar racing, ski, read, and ride her motorcycle. She lives in Indianapolis with her husband, her daughter, and their dog.